Come Unto Me

The Lives and Stories of Those Who Met Jesus

Come Unto Me

The Lives and Stories of Those Who Met Jesus

PHILIP D. PATTERSON

COLLEGE PRESS PUBLISHING CO., Joplin, Mo.

Library of Congress Catalog Card Number:93-70674
International Standard Book Number:0-89900-613-2

Artwork
by
Kevin Thomas

Table of Contents

Introduction

As I was reading the Scriptures recently, it occurred to me that the people whose stories are recorded in the Bible are as historical as our Savior. I had always believed in an historical Jesus, with an earthly family. I believed that he had called out real-life apostles. And I realized that Pilate and Herod and some of the officials in Acts were historically verifiable characters.

But I had a view of the masses of people who came to Jesus in the Gospel accounts as coming from some biblical "central casting." Some were lame or blind and demon-possessed. Some were humble, others were self-righteous. Some were sinners, others were honest and good.

Yet, they seemed to have neither a past nor a future. They remain forever frozen in time in their lone recorded interaction with Jesus. I would read their stories as if their sole reason for existence was to further the story line of the Gospels to its inevitable conclusion at the empty tomb.

Then it dawned on me. These "minor" characters in the Scriptures are not only historical, they even have living descendants, sixty generations removed, walking the earth today, grappling with the same issues that brought their ancestors to Christ so many years ago. The ones who loved Him have living ancestors today. The ones who plotted against Him also have their progeny.

I began to wonder if I had an ancestor in the Bible. And like Alex Haley tracing his genealogical roots to Africa, I began to comb the Gospels in search of my spiritual ancestor.

After searching, I think I found one in the man who brought his demon-possessed boy to Jesus in the ninth chapter of Mark. In a moment of self-revealing candor he said, "I do believe; help me overcome my unbelief!" When I read that passage for perhaps the hundredth time, this time looking for my "roots," I knew I had found them. Here was someone in the very presence of Jesus who wanted to believe in his heart what his head told him couldn't be true.

In my search I found many other interesting characters. After reading their stories, I had many questions. What were these people like? How did they hear of the Master? What led them to seek out Jesus? What happened to them after their interaction with Him? Why were they singled out from the masses who came to Jesus for teaching and healing? Why was their story recorded by the writers of the Gospels?

This book attempts to give some plausible and inspirational answers to these questions. It is part history and part fiction. In the book are stories of people who sought out Jesus to have their sicknesses healed or their sins forgiven. Other stories tell of people whom Jesus sought out to teach and to heal. The book will show that the needs of those seekers nearly 2,000 years ago are not unlike our needs today. I hope it also shows that our Lord, Who seeks and knocks and waits, is the same forever. The common theme of the stories in the book is that a life touched by the Master is never the same afterwards. I hope that in some way, your life will be touched by Him through these stories.

Some final notes of clarification and a few "thank you's" belong here as well. In the stories that follow, all of the phrases in quotations are taken directly from the *New International Version* of the Scriptures. In some instances I took verses from different Gospel accounts and blended then into a single narrative, but no sentence appears in quotes unless it came from the text.

One variance has been made from the quoted text. All nouns and pronouns referring to Jesus are capitalized, regardless of whether the NIV did so. This is for clarity and consistency with the rest of the manuscript. Many of the individuals in these stories have no recorded names, and I never supplied one. By capitalizing each reference to Jesus, I let the reader know when pronouns refer to Him and when they refer to one who is interacting with Jesus.

Many people have helped along the way with this manuscript, some intentionally and some unknowingly. I read the *Daily Study Bible* by William Barclay and found richer meaning in these old, familiar stories. I sat in the audience and listened as the characters in the Scriptures came alive thanks to such speakers as Tim Martin, Jeff Walling, Ed Enzor, Terry Rush, Ken Jones and Ronnie White. You have helped me with your insight, even without being aware of it, and I thank you now. Others helped directly, including my "unofficial" editors, Jeanine Varner, and Bob Ross; my "official" editor, John Hunter; and my secretary, Susie Rodman. I am grateful to call these three co-workers my friends.

But most of all, I owe a debt of gratitude in this project to my wife, Linda. She encouraged me to write the first stories for a ladies' retreat she organized in 1990, and then encouraged me to expand them further, always reminding me to write from the heart and not just the head. It is to her credit that this book has been written and it is to her that it is dedicated.

Philip D. Patterson
January, 1993

The Samaritan woman at the well.

Chapter One

Breaking Down the Walls

The animosity between the Arabs and Jews is as modern as this morning's newspaper and as ancient as Isaac and Ishmael. In this story, Jesus breaks the traditional walls of His day between nations and between genders and takes His message to a surprised Samaritan woman.

But the greatest wall He broke down on this day was the one that kept the Samaritans from worshiping in the temple. He didn't do it by pushing Samaritans into the temple, but by pulling God out of it. Of course, God had never been trapped in any temple made by man, but the Jews of the day thought He was.

Even today, as I sit in my familiar pew, singing familiar songs and fellowshipping with my friends, I sometimes forget that my congregation, so friendly in appearance to me, can be a strange and foreboding place to a visitor. Jesus said that the only walls that define true churches are the walls of spirit and truth. When we add the walls of tradition or preference, we're

*no different from the Pharisees who hung the "Not Welcome"
sign on the temple for hundreds of years.*

The well was not the nearest to the residents of
Sychar. And at a depth of more than one hundred feet, it
wasn't as convenient as the percolating springs in town.

But you could always be assured of privacy at the
well outside of town. And the woman who was carrying her huge clay pot on her head to the well in the midday sun cherished the privacy more than convenience.
It's tough to be stuck in a small town when you have a
bad reputation, and her private life was among the most
talked about in town.

As she neared the well, she passed a band of men,
about twelve in number. They were Jews. Must be in a
hurry, she thought, for the only Jews who came through
Samaria were the ones in a hurry.

Samaria was simultaneously next to—and a world
apart from—the two regions where the Jews lived. It
bordered Judea in the south and Galilee in the north,
both inhabited by the Jews.

The quickest way to make the journey between the
two regions was to go directly through Samaria.

But most Jews loathed taking this route. The Samaritans were lower than dogs to them. Any contact with a
Samaritan made one ceremonially impure, and one of
the prime reasons for travel between the regions was to
celebrate religious holidays. Why risk contact with a
dog on your way to worship?

Therefore, most Jewish travelers crossed the Jordan,
traveled its east bank and crossed it again to arrive at

their destination without going through Samaria. The two boat trips and the longer route added a day to the journey, but it was a day that most Jewish travelers were happy to spend.

So it was a curious sight to see this band of men traveling into town. She had stared when she approached them, and she felt them looking back at her even after they had passed. Up ahead, at the well, she could see that they had left one behind. She had wanted privacy, but, better a stranger, even a Jew, than someone from town.

Jesus sat at the well resting from the morning's walk. It was noon, and they had arrived at the fork of the road at the place known as "Jacob's well." Jesus knew the stories of the land from His childhood. The land had been purchased by Jacob, who bequeathed it on his deathbed to Joseph. Years later, Joseph, as he was dying in Egypt, requested to be buried in the land his father had given him.

It was an area rich in Jewish history, but now largely avoided by Jews. It had been the home of the Samaritans since the days of Assyrian captivity. About 750 years earlier the Assyrians had captured the northern kingdom where Jesus was heading on this day. They had taken many of the Jews away and repatriated the area with people from other cultures in an attempt to dilute the influence of the ones left behind.

So the Samaritans had become the inhabitants of some of the most treasured parcels of Jewish land. Jesus had come to the region on His way north to Galilee because the Pharisees in Judea were making trouble over His apostles' practice of baptizing His believers. He knew that at this stage in His ministry He didn't need a confrontation with the Pharisees. There was much left to do, and they would be waiting for Him when He returned. That much was certain.

Jesus watched with interest as the woman approached Him. Towns were built around springs, yet this woman was coming to a travelers' well that required a long rope and a heavy pull to get the same water that rose to the surface in the town.

He said nothing as she went about her task of lowering her small pitcher into the well several times to fill the larger jar. The apostles had faded from view by the time she had filled her jar.

When she finished, He asked, "Will you give me a drink?"

Though she was aware of His presence, she had not expected that He would speak to her. He was a Jew, she was a Samaritan. He was probably the leader of the group that was going into town. Since almost all Jewish pilgrimages through this area were religious ones, she surmised that He must be the Rabbi of the group, despite His youth. No Rabbi spoke to a woman in public, especially a Samaritan one.

She was shocked into silence for a moment, then mumbled her reply. "You are a Jew and I am a Samaritan woman. How can you ask me for a drink?"

Seven centuries of animosity lay behind her surprise. The Samaritans had intermarried with the northern Jews left behind and had even built a temple in Mount Gerizim in which Jewish Samaritans could worship. But the southern Jews, who had been carried as a whole into Babylonian captivity (and had never given up their racial purity) never accepted the Samaritan Jews. At one point, they declared a holy war on the Samaritans and destroyed the Mount Gerizim temple. More than 150 years after that war, the hard feelings still remained.

He began to teach her as she gave Him a drink. She listened as he spoke of "living water" and eternal life. In jest, she had asked for some of that water so she could stop her daily treks to the well. He was more of a heretic than a madman, she thought as she took the cup back from Him.

"Go get your husband and come back," He said.

The request caught her by surprise. "I have no husband," she said, carefully covering her face with her veil and hurrying her preparations to leave.

"You are right to say you have no husband," He said. "The fact is, you have had five husbands, and the man you now have is not your husband. What you said is quite true."

How could He have known! She felt her eye quickly. It was still a little tender, but it was no longer puffy, and the purple color had finally left the day before. He couldn't have guessed her sorry home life by her appearance. And He hadn't been in town, so He couldn't have heard the rumors. Yet He knew her lie.

This was uncomfortable territory. It's difficult to become suddenly transparent when what's inside is so ugly.

Her mind raced. He's at least a rabbi, she thought. Probably a prophet as well. Think of a theological question. Any question. Just get Him off the subject. In the distance loomed the mountain. That would do.

"Sir, I can see You are a prophet. Our fathers worshiped on this mountain, but you Jews claim that the place where we must worship is in Jerusalem."

That should do, she thought. He'll debate this for a while. I'll take my jar and get away from this man who knows everything I ever did. I can do better taking ridicule at the spring in town. At least the lies work there.

But His answer stopped her. Instead of giving her the centuries old line about "God's people," He said something that made sense.

"Believe Me, woman, a time is coming when you will worship the Father neither on this mountain nor in Jerusalem."

Was this a Rabbi saying that worship could occur somewhere other than Jerusalem? Who was He? His words said He was a heretic, but His insight into her home life said He was a prophet. She put down the jar. Whoever He was, she was now intrigued by what He had to say.

"You Samaritans worship what you do not know; we worship what we do know, for salvation is from the Jews."

She started to stiffen. He had sounded so different at first, but she had heard this before.

"Yet a time is coming and has now come when the true worshippers will worship the Father in Spirit and in truth, for they are the kind of worshippers the Father seeks. God is spirit, and His worshippers must worship in spirit and in truth."

The trip had been quick for the apostles. The Samaritan merchants didn't talk much with Jewish travelers, and the Twelve weren't comfortable talking with them either. They had made their purchases quickly and walked away with the hurried pace of ones being watched.

When they could see Jesus, they were surprised to see that the same woman they had met on their way to town was sitting at His feet. They began to argue among themselves about who should tell Him that encounters like this were out of the question for a Teacher of His stature. None of them, however, agreed to be the one to speak up.

She remembered the stories from when she was a little girl being taken to the temple on Mount Gerizim by her half-Jewish father. Though those journeys now seemed far removed from her current life, she could still remember the beautiful Jewish word for the One who was to come: "Messiah." She would ask His opinion about the One to come.

"I know that Messiah is coming. When He comes, He will explain everything to us."

"I Who speak to you am He," Jesus said.

She scrambled to her feet and ran towards the town, leaving her jar behind, and passing the surprised band of Jews now approaching them. She knew she had to tell someone, anyone. She always avoided social contact whenever possible. She was the scorned one in this little gossiping community. But now, she had found the Messiah, and she would risk the ridicule of the town to tell the story.

He would stay for two days in the town. Many of the Samaritans would believe and be immersed by the apostles in the town's springs. But none would feel so clean as the woman who once went outside the town for her water.

CHAPTER TWO

"God Has Come to Help His People"

"Give me liberty or give me death!" "Death before dishonor!" "Back to the Bible!"

Ever notice how some words just seem made for rallying cries? Lengthy speeches have their place in democracy and in theology, yet it's the simple phrases that move the public to act.

Such a cry is found in this story. Jesus has just performed a miracle, raising the son of the widow of Nain from the dead. And the people spread the word: "God has come to help His people!"

"God has come to help His people!" What a cry!

They could have called out, "God has come to organize His people!" but I doubt that it would have stirred much emotion. Some rallying cries are just better than others.

And "God has come to help His people!" is still our rallying cry today. We serve a God who served us first. Paul calls Him a king who conquers and gives gifts to the conquered

rather than extracting tribute as was the custom.
God has always helped His people, even in their darkest hours, and that is the message of the story below.

The funeral procession was approaching the city gate. From there, they would turn left and walk a little less than a mile to the burial grounds outside the city. The young man being carried to his burial had been healthy three days ago. But a threshing accident had left him severely wounded in the field, and he had lost too much blood to survive.

His mother had been summoned when he was first injured, and she had held his hand during the final minutes before his last breath. The next three days had been a blur, and her friends, recognizing her state of shock, had made most of the funeral arrangements for her. Even now, as she walked, she held the steady gaze of one not fully aware of what was happening.

Perhaps the shock was a merciful thing, for her future was bleak. Widowed more than ten years earlier, she had depended on her son, an only child, for support, and he had always provided it. Now she was alone.

Her son had readily taken over as head of the household when his father died, even though he was only sixteen at the time. Though they didn't own much, he and his mother had gotten by on his earnings from hard labor in the fields. They had hoped someday to buy a farm and hire workers of their own. His mother always reminded him that the time would come when he would not be young and strong, and that they must save for the future. But it seemed to take all their earnings just to get by, and their modest savings had just been spent on the boy's burial costs.

Now his mother was a widow without family or any means of support. But she wasn't thinking about that as the procession went through the gate. She couldn't worry about the future when her heart was breaking over the present.

Jesus and His apostles were approaching Nain from Capernaum, where He had healed the servant of a Roman centurion. The Twelve had been apprehensive of any dealings with the Roman government, and they were nervous about the encounter with the centurion, a Roman army captain in charge of one hundred men.

They hadn't actually seen the man—he had sent others to do his asking for him while he stayed at the bedside of the servant. First came a party of Jews who vouched for his character, followed a party of his Roman friends. The second group requested that Jesus not even trouble Himself with going to the house of the centurion, who felt unworthy of a visit from Jesus. Instead, they asked Him to heal the servant from a distance. This request sent a sigh of relief through the apostles, who wanted little contact with the Roman authorities.

When the report came back from the house that the servant was well by the time the second party returned, the apostles were ready to clear out of the area. Among the Twelve were Simon, who was a Zealot, an outlaw party of known haters of Romans, and Matthew, who had walked away from his job as a tax collector for Rome, giving no prior notice. Jesus, however, showed neither fear nor deference to the Romans. He seemed to treat all people the same, they observed. He had even commented on the great faith of the centurion, who knew that Jesus could heal the servant from a distance.

As usual, the teachings and miracles in Capernaum had drawn a crowd, and many followers were still with Jesus and His apostles as they approached Nain. When they saw the procession exit the town gate, the crowd instinctively halted—some out of respect, and some out of a distaste for becoming ceremonially unclean from coming near a dead body.

Jesus, however, kept walking. He saw the widow and grieved for her. Approaching the procession alone, He walked directly to her, took her hand and said, "Don't cry." He laid His hand on the coffin and asked the ones carrying it to stand still.

Following Jewish tradition, the coffin was being carried with the lid off for all to see the body. The injury that had taken his life was scarcely noticeable after the applying of the wrappings and spices.

Taking the young man's hand, in a loud voice, Jesus said, "Young man, I say to you, get up!"

The widow looked at Jesus in amazement. Who is this madman, she thought. Who has come to interrupt this burial? How cruel and insensitive! But before she could utter a protest, her son sat up in his coffin and began to speak. His first words were to ask for his mother, whom Jesus led to the side of the coffin.

The crowds began to shout. Some said, "A great prophet has appeared among us!" Others, recognizing that this was not the work of an ordinary prophet, shouted, "God has come to help His people!"

Around the countryside the cry went, "God has come to help His people!" The very idea of a helper-God was radically different from what they were being taught by the Pharisees and Sadducees. They had heard of a God who would come to *judge* His people. They had prayed for a God who would come to *rule* His people. They were wary of a God who would come to *punish* His people. But here was God—in the form of a man—who had come to *help* His people. Not to organize, not to conquer, but to help. From the least in the eyes of the world, like the widow of Nain, to the greatest, like the centurion, God had come to help His people.

The widow's gift.

CHAPTER THREE

THE BIGGEST GIFT OF ALL

"It's the thought that counts." It's one of our culture's acceptable lies that has endured because we want so badly to believe it. It's used whenever a gift is too small, too late or totally inappropriate. It was what our parents said when we brought home ugly handmade ornaments for the Christmas tree.

But we all know the truth: the size of a gift does count to most of us. Engagement rings are measured in carats, sports cars in horsepower. You name it, and there's a way to tell if your gift is the biggest and the most expensive.

Jesus saw through this fallacy. In the story below, Jesus observed a gift that hardly registered on the scale, but was the largest gift of all in His sight. The widow could have chosen to not give the gift at all, yet she knew that while God didn't need her gift, He wanted her heart, and this gift came from the heart.

Have you ever given God something you really needed? Of

course you could have spent some of the money you put in the offering, but did you ever sacrifice in order to give? In bringing her gift to the temple, the widow was risking starvation as well as humiliation—two conditions most of us prefer to avoid. Yet the beatitudes indicate that God sees nothing wrong with humble and hungry people. While others gave a gift of money, the widow gave a gift of faith in the story below.

Today was the day of giving at the temple in Jerusalem. People would come from miles around bearing their gifts of gold, jewelry, and other goods to lay at the feet of the priest.

Over the years, a tradition of giving had developed. At the front of the temple were thirteen collection boxes, each dedicated to a different type of gift, such as coins, firewood for the altar, jewelry, etc. All gifts were given openly for all to see, with the largest gifts being given first, in the hopes that others would imitate the larger givers in their gifts.

For many, the act was not as much a sacrifice as a public display of net worth. Since most devout Jews tithed, one's profits from the previous season could be easily measured by his gift to the temple treasury. And since many Jews held the view that God rewarded men monetarily for good deeds, and punished them physically for evil deeds, giving large gifts was a public way for the rich to display how God had favored them for righteous living.

The widow knew all this as she prepared to take her gift. She would be last—there was little doubt about that. Her two copper coins were called "lepta" by the Greeks, meaning "thin ones." These smallest of coins individually were worth 1/16th of a penny. She would have to walk last up to the box for collecting currency. It was shaped like a trumpet set on its horn, with the coins dropped into the mouthpiece. And with all those watching who had already given, she would give the smallest gift of all. Yet it was all she had.

It hadn't always been like this. During his life, her husband had been a silversmith, and their gifts had always been from the finest of his work. Yet, when he died, she could not carry on the trade, and could only find domestic work in the houses of the rich to sustain her. She and her husband had no children, and her husband had no brothers to claim her as a wife under the Levirate law. She had fallen through the cracks of a society that had little value for single women with no marketable skills. In a matter of months, she had gone from a place of prominence in the line of the givers to the last position.

But she always gave, even out of her poverty. No matter that the amount was so insignificant it could not even buy a dove for sacrifice, she gave. Somehow, she had never felt comfortable with the system when she and her husband were prominently escorted to the front of the line with their gifts of ornate silver. And now, oddly, when she was giving the least, she felt the most at peace. For her gift went far beyond the tithe that the others were giving. Her gift, as small as it seemed, represented her entire earthly wealth.

So, as on every giving day, she dressed and left her house, coins clutched tightly in her hand. Then she waited, while the others showed publicly how good

God had been to them. Today the wait took even longer than usual, as the approach of Passover signaled a renewed interest in giving for many. The helpers of the priest were busy outside the temple, ordering the line to reflect the size of the gift. More than once, she had to carefully whisper the size of her gift to a helper who would look quizzically at her as if to say, "Why bother?"

She bothered to give because she knew it was right. Her ancestors had suffered far more at the hands of the Egyptians, the Babylonians and the Assyrians than she was suffering in the grip of poverty. If her ancestors had given solely from their wealth, she reasoned, this temple would not be standing today.

Finally it was her turn. She was skillful in walking down the aisle avoiding eye contact with any who were watching. Fortunately, on this day, most of the rich had long since lost interest in the dwindling gifts and had retreated to their homes. Ahead was the priest, looking grateful that the end of the line had come at last. Years of experience had taught him that the first ten percent of the givers contributed ninety percent of the temple's treasury. All of the donors after that, and there were many, were almost superfluous to the work of the temple. Yet they must be encouraged, too. It was all a part of the job.

The priest had come to recognize the widow over the months as a regular contributor, and more importantly to him, as the end of the line. So, with a smile of relief, he greeted her as she walked down the aisle.

But on this day, a small group of men were gathered

at the side of the thirteen boxes. One was speaking to the others as she walked up. Her interest had been drawn to His conversation as she heard Him condemn the rich for their showy ways in the synagogue and in the temple while they privately devoured widows' houses. She knew that someday soon she would be evicted from her home. She had not made a payment in the months since her husband's death, and she was not likely to make one soon. "Such men will be punished most severely," she heard Him say. She certainly hoped that was true, as she walked forward to give.

Reaching as far into the box as possible, so that the small coins might not be so conspicuous, she dropped them. But, as always, the gift was announced by one of the helpers stationed by the coin box. "Two lepta," he announced to the small number left in the temple.

"Two lepta!" The words burned like a brand as she turned to walk away. But as she turned, the Man who was speaking earlier about the wealthy spoke again. This time, He was talking about her.

"I tell you the truth," He said, "this poor widow has put in more than all the others." His voice was authoritative and firm, causing all who were left in the temple to stop and listen.

"All these people gave their gifts out of their wealth," He said, gesturing to the earlier givers. "But she, out of her poverty, put in all she had to live on."

With that, the wealthy began to exit the temple, muttering as they went, while the priest hurriedly retired to his quarters to avoid confronting the issues of wealth and justice with this radical teacher. But the widow remained. For the first time since her husband's death, someone had seen through her poverty and made her feel worthy. She heard someone speak His name, and she realized that this was the Teacher she had heard so much about.

As she stayed and listened, Jesus talked about the beautiful temple that surrounded them, and how it would be a heap of rubble within one generation. He ended with an admonition: "Be always on the watch and pray that you may be able to stand before the Son of Man."

Finally, it was time to go. As she walked out alone, she took another look at the temple and its ornamentation. "Not one stone left on another," He had said. All these people who stood in line today to impress others were giving for nothing, she thought.

But she remembered what else He had said. For some, there was another line that would form—the line to stand before God. And in that line, the order would be determined not by the size of the gift, but by the size of the heart.

CHAPTER FOUR

A HOLE IN THE ROOF IS A WINDOW TO THE SOUL

There's an old fable about a crowd that waited for hours to see a processional of the king and his court. Shortly before the anticipated moment, however, off to the side two dogs began to fight. Many in the crowd, bored with the wait, turned to watch the dogfight for diversion. At precisely that moment the king passed by. They had exchanged the opportunity to partake in the majesty of the king for the momentary distraction of the dogfight.

There's an interesting story in the Gospels where Martha frets about her house and the meal while Mary sits at the feet of her Savior. It seems that Martha saw the sideshow, while Mary seized the opportunity to savor the procession.

How often do we do something similar to the onlookers in the fable? The next time I'm tempted to hurry through my Sunday worship to watch my favorite football team, or crowd my devotional time to watch the news, I hope I remember that fable.

The story that follows is an apocryphal spin on a true happening. We all know someone like the character in this story. You can find them watching the dogfight and missing the King.

His was a nice house. A spacious one, too, one of the largest in Capernaum. It faced the east and let in the morning light, a quality one looked for in a good home. It had a cobblestone path to the door and all the appropriate messages attached to the frame of the door to mark it as a proper Jewish home. But what marked it the most was the roof—a red tile roof. The hard baked clay not only kept out the wind and the rain, it stood as a symbol that this was a house of a wealthy man. Not just any structure could hold the weight of such a permanent roof, and not just any pocketbook could afford the painstaking production and placement of the tiles across the beams by the workmen.

Other homes around had roofs of thatch or straw that smelled and leaked when wet with the early morning dew. Their porous quality made it impossible to keep warmth in the house, and they easily caught fire.

Today, however, the owner of this fine house had another reason to be proud: Jesus was under his roof. He had come to Capernaum early in the day, and, seeing the crowds and the heat, He had chosen this house as a place to teach the host of people while escaping the midday sun. Out of all of the houses in town, his was the one that was to be blessed by a visit from the Master. Perhaps this would get him the respect he hungered for.

The crowd was an unusual mix, even for the type of

crowds who followed the Teacher, for on this day, Pharisees and teachers of the law from every village of Galilee and the entire region of Judea were there. Even the learned men of Jerusalem had come out, a fact that pleased the owner of the house nearly as much as the fact that Jesus had chosen his house for a podium.

Of course the crowd contained the usual sick and lame. Hardly any way to keep them out, thought the owner. Wherever the Teacher went, He attracted them by the scores as they came looking for healing. But it never hurt to keep your eyes on those who came for healing. They might be likely to steal something on their way out, the owner thought. And with a crowd as thick as this one, who could ever finger just which one had done it? Well, that's just the price you pay for the notoriety of hosting the Teacher, he thought. He only wished that some of the poorest of them had washed before entering the rapidly filling house.

When the house could hold absolutely no more people, the crowd gathered at the door and at every window. The large eastern window that let in so much light a little while ago was now crammed with followers of Jesus straining to hear His every word. But all those people were making his spacious home look dark and crowded, the owner thought. The ones in the windows and doors were blocking all the breeze and most of the light, yet the crowd seemed so mesmerized by the message and the miracles and the way Jesus handled the questions of the teachers of the law that no one but the owner noticed that they were destroying his home.

Suddenly, the darkness of the room got a little lighter.

A shaft of light shone down directly on Jesus' head. At first it seemed that this might be one of those supernatural lights—like the one that those who had been at the river when Jesus was baptized recalled seeing. But, to the horror of the owner, this was just ordinary sunlight let in by a hole left by a tile that had been dislodged from the roof. And worse, someone was up there dislodging another!

"Man! What are you doing?" he cried out involuntarily. Immediately he began to blush, because he had interrupted the Master. Those silly zombie-like followers had been so wrapped up in the message that they hadn't even noticed the shaft of light yet. He had to say something quickly to explain his outburst. His cheeks burned and he fumbled for words in a mouth that was suddenly dry.

"My roof," he said half-heartedly, pointing to the hole and looking for a sympathetic listener in the crowd somewhere. "They're tearing a hole in my roof. Get a guard!"

The whole crowd was looking up at the ever-widening hole that now revealed that at least four men were on his roof, each pulling tiles off from a different direction. Yet the followers only watched with curiosity, and no one moved to stop the men, an impossible task anyway since even those in the doorway were pinned in by the crowd outside looking in. Didn't they know how expensive that roof was?

Worse still, Jesus didn't rebuke the men. He stood and watched as the hole quickly became as long as the body of a man and about twice as wide. At that point, the vandals stood and disappeared from the hole. They had come to get a look at the famous Teacher and now they were leaving.

"Stop!" the owner cried. And for the second time in the span of a few moments, he felt the embarrassment of scores of eyes on him. "They're getting away! Call someone!" he said in a pleading voice. Again he sought understanding from the eyes but found none. What did they know about expensive roofs? Except for the important ones from Jerusalem, probably none of them had ever even been under a tiled roof before, let alone paid for one.

But to the ones who knew the cost of a tiled roof, he had embarrassed himself even more, and he knew it. He had shown the measure of his worth by showing his distress at the removing of the tiles. Those who could truly afford a tile roof could afford to repair one as well. It was the wealthy ones from Jerusalem who were really pitying him right now, and he felt their pity in their silence.

In his anger and self-pity, the owner had not seen the paralytic until he was just above the head of Jesus. To his amazement, the men had reappeared with a mat and four ropes and were lowering a paralytic through the hole in the roof to the floor by Jesus. People shifted and moved while the overcrowded room became even more crowded to make room for the mat. The last child scurried to the left of Jesus just as the mat touched the floor. The friends on the roof dropped their ropes in faith that they would be needed no more, and began crawling off the roof.

Jesus smiled at the helpers as they left the hole and then looked down at the paralytic. "Friend, your sins are forgiven," He said. The statement brought frowns to the faces of the Pharisees and teachers of the law. They began to whisper among themselves. The owner of the house hadn't been listening to Jesus, and he was sure the Pharisees were talking about him and his petulant behavior over the roof.

But Jesus read the situation differently. "Why are you thinking these things in your hearts?" He asked. "Which is easier: to say, 'Your sins are forgiven' or to say 'Get up and walk'? But that you may know the Son of Man has authority on earth to forgive sins," Turning now His attention from the frowning Pharisees who knew all too well what was coming, "I tell you, get up, take up your mat and go home."

As the man arose, with the shaky motions of a newborn calf finding its legs for the first time, the crowd began to rejoice and praise God. The Pharisees and teachers of the law exited immediately: they would have to fight this blasphemer another day. It was time to get back to Jerusalem and begin to discredit the story before it could get to the city.

The healed man quickly obeyed the command of Jesus and rolled up his mat, wrapped the four ropes around it and parted the crowd as he leaped into the streets to tell others of his good fortune.

The crowd was quick to follow, full of praise and awe at the remarkable events of the day, leaving the owner alone. His moment of glory had turned to one of embarrassment. The men he had openly rebuked and wanted to arrest were regarded by the crowd, and even by the Teacher, as heroes. In fact, the Teacher had remarked about the faith of the friends being as great as that of the paralytic right before He healed the man.

The owner of the fine home surveyed the damage. A couple of broken chairs and a torn curtain in the eastern window were evidence of the huge crowd that had virtually vanished with the healed man. And as he looked around, the owner realized that while he had hosted the Master *under* his roof, all he had worried about was his roof.

The next day would bring two pieces of bad news. First, the roof would cost almost as much to repair as it had originally cost to build. Second, the Teacher had visited one other home in the town the previous day after the miracle: the home of Levi the tax collector.

Nicodemus enters the house to see Jesus.

CHAPTER FIVE

VISITING THE LIGHT IN THE DARK OF NIGHT

He was an enigma then, and he remains one today. Scholars for centuries have puzzled over Nicodemus. What was his motivation for his late night visit with Jesus? What happened afterwards? Within a few years after the close of the Scriptures, many variant stories existed about his life after the encounter with Jesus.

This much we know. He wanted to know more about Jesus, yet he didn't want anyone to see him come or go. He was taught of the new birth directly by Jesus, yet we have no record that he was born again. He used his position in the Sanhedrin to defend Jesus at one point (John 7:50-52) but was strangely absent in the account of the martyrdom of Stephen at the hands of the same body. He doesn't appear during the trial or crucifixion of Jesus, yet he came later, bringing spices for the burial (John 19:39).

In short, he was like most of us. Sometimes courageous, sometimes afraid. Wanting to believe yet nagged by doubts.

In this story, we look at what his first encounter with Jesus might have been like.

His name meant "victor over the people," and by his status he was certainly that. For Nicodemus was not only a Pharisee, he was a member of the Sanhedrin, the ruling body of Judaism. But tonight he looked and felt like anything but a victor of the people. Tonight he crept in the dark, hugging the walls of strange houses to avoid being seen. The eliteness of Sanhedrin membership had its advantages, but it also had its disadvantages, and being easily recognized was one.

He sought the Teacher who had come to Jerusalem to observe the Passover feast. Just a few days before the celebration, He had sent ripples through the religious community when He had entered the temple courtyard and acted like a madman, according to ones who were there. He had called the temple "My Father's house," and had told the sellers of sheep, cattle and doves to get out. He had turned over their tables and even brandished a whip at those who tried to challenge Him. The money had flown everywhere, and the street urchins and beggars had gotten away with quite a bit of it.

That display of righteous indignation intrigued Nicodemus. Surely the Teacher had known that the system of selling sacrifices in the temple had developed out of necessity. No one seemed to have the time to prearrange these things, so an entire industry had developed to make acceptable sacrifices easily available with a minimum of, well, sacrifice. Maybe the hawkers and barkers sometimes were overeager. He could hear their incessant cries in the courtyard below when he sat in the chambers of the Sanhedrin. Yes, they were annoying, but they filled a needed function in the busy Jewish society of Jerusalem and had always been tolerated until the one named Jesus had driven them out.

Nicodemus had heard about His teachings and His miracles; now he wanted to meet the Teacher Himself. But since Jesus was beginning to accumulate some powerful enemies, he felt it best to do his visiting under the cover of darkness. So, here he was, "victor of the people," looking for a house in a part of town whose sounds and smells he didn't even comprehend, more than two hours after sundown. He had heard that the Teacher ate and stayed with commoners. Now his offended senses confirmed it. Nicodemus was out of his element here. Were the stares that he felt real or imagined? Curious or threatening?

He did find one comfort in the part of the city where the Teacher was staying: these people wouldn't recognize a member of the Sanhedrin. However, the thieves could spot a rich man, and that was his primary fear now.

But here it was, the house. His knock was immediately answered by a large man. His rough hands and weathered face proclaimed the time he had spent in the salt breeze of the sea. Nicodemus expected this. He had been told that the Teacher had surrounded himself with fishermen, tax collectors and the like.

Fortunately, the ones in the outer room had received his message and the Teacher was expecting him. He didn't feel like explaining his presence to this group.

He was escorted into the simple room where the Teacher would soon sleep. Surveying the small room, Nicodemus realized that his servants would sleep in better quarters tonight. For a moment he thought of offering the Teacher better accommodations at his home, but he remembered that this was an unofficial visit. He surely couldn't take the "evidence" home with him.

Jesus was younger than Nicodemus had imagined. About the size he imagined, but younger. Not particularly handsome. No, it wasn't His appearance or size that was attracting the crowds.

But while he was assessing Jesus, Nicodemus realized that Jesus was assessing him. He also realized that if someone was to break the silence it would have to be him. He had heard that the Teacher seemed to know what was in a man's heart before he even spoke, and looking into those eyes he believed it. In fact, he could feel it, and it felt uncomfortable. If Nicodemus wanted a conversation, he knew he'd better ask a question fast. He blurted one out, getting right to the point.

"Rabbi, we know You are a teacher who has come from God. For no one could perform the miraculous signs you are doing if God were not with Him."

The "we" in the question surprised even Nicodemus. He was on a personal mission, yet he felt compelled to act as if he carried the question for others. He sat hoping that Jesus wouldn't press him on who the "we" was. He was now more nervous than he had been as he sneaked through the streets of Jerusalem.

Jesus nodded. He, of course, had heard it before. The

signs, always the signs. When would they understand the message?

He spoke to the common people in parables. He talked to them of crops and fruit trees, lost coins and found sheep and made applications from the stories. But now He was speaking to a learned leader of the Jews. He would use a slightly deeper metaphor with Nicodemus to test him.

"I tell you the truth, unless a man is born again, he cannot see the kingdom of God."

What a strange statement, Nicodemus thought. His reply was an immediate, half-startled one. "How can a man be born when he is old? Surely he cannot enter a second time into his mother's womb to be born!"

Jesus had His answer. The learned elite of the Jews would come no closer to understanding the spiritual nature of His message than the unlearned masses. And possibly, their learning would even get in the way.

After explaining the spiritual nature of the second birth, He took a page from Jewish history to predict His death: "Just as Moses lifted up the snake in the desert, so the Son of Man must be lifted up that everyone who believes in Him may have eternal life."

He spoke some more, but Nicodemus was having trouble with these strange teachings. A second birth? A Savior lifted up on a stick like the brass serpent? When Jesus got to the part about men preferring the dark instead of the light, Nicodemus blushed. He preferred the dark himself tonight. And in a few moments, Nicodemus, the "victor over the people," was going to excuse himself. He would shroud himself in the twin cloaks of darkness and tradition to return to his life as a member of the ruling class.

Only later, after the reports of the empty tomb, did Nicodemus understand: the second birth first requires a death.

Chapter Six

Feeding the Puppies

In Hebrews I read that "He rewards those who earnestly seek Him," yet I don't recall searching too hard to find Jesus. It seems He's always been there.

I didn't have to walk a day's journey into the countryside to find Him. I didn't have to be carried to Him or led by the hand to Him. He was a part of my upbringing, going back several generations.

For me, and others in my situation, it would have been more of a challenge to avoid finding Him. Is that passage in Hebrews meant for a twentieth century generation that has the Bible on computer and the Gospels on videotape?

I'm convinced that the passage in Hebrews is not only about learning of the existence of Jesus, it's also about learning of the character of Jesus.

Just as the earnest seeking of Jesus by the woman in this story was rewarded, He still rewards His seekers today with more insight into His unique nature.

The psalmist wrote, "Be still, and know that I am God." It's the being still that's the hardest part of getting to know Him, and that's why the Hebrews passage is still relevant today. The diligence required of a modern-day seeker is different from the diligence required of the woman in this story, but the reward is the same: we find Jesus and He gives us healing.

"Lord, Son of David, have mercy on me!" the woman at His feet cried. She was a Canaanite woman from the area of Tyre, noted for its animosity towards Jews.

The Twelve had been with Jesus for nearly three years, yet this was their first trip outside the borders of Palestine. Wishing to get away from the pressing crowds and the badgering Pharisees, Jesus had retreated outside the borders of Galilee into the land of the Canaanites to the north.

As they had traveled north, the apostles had puzzled over His motivation. Was He fleeing His enemies? Was He tiring of the demands of the crowds? Why Tyre? Why not a more friendly region?

Often Jesus would take them out into the countryside or out onto a boat to escape the crowds, but never had they left the borders of the country for rest. In a search for plausible explanations, the apostles had whispered among themselves. Was there a plot? Were they in danger? Yet none of them asked the Master why He journeyed so far to the north for this time of rest. *"Lord, Son of David, have mercy on me! My daughter is suffering terribly from demon possession,"* she repeated.

Leaving the borders of Palestine, the apostles had felt a sense of relief and apprehension simultaneously. Their apprehension came from the fact that they were not accustomed to being outside their own borders, and this was not a particularly friendly environment for their first taste of international travel. The relief, though, off-set the anxiety. They were thrilled to be out of the juris-diction of the Pharisees and high priests. Their last encounter with them had been over whether the apostles washed their hands before eating.

Many of the apostles hadn't even been aware that they were breaking a rule in sitting to eat with unwashed hands, and most of them agreed that it would be better to do it than to risk the wrath of the religious elite over such a small thing. They had watched anxiously as He had argued with them. The Master never seemed to share their willingness to accommodate the Pharisees when He thought they were wrong.

And instead of talking about hand washing, Jesus had attacked the Pharisees on hypocrisy and accused them of being the ones who were unclean. The apostles were certain that they were headed for immediate trou-ble, yet the Pharisees had left. They would be back, however.

Later, they had asked Him, "Do you know that the Pharisees were offended when they heard this?" He had called them "blind guides" leading men into pits. He had called Peter "dull" when he didn't understand the allegory.

"Don't you see that whatever enters the mouth goes into the stomach and then out of the body? But the things that come out of the mouth come from the heart, and these make a man 'unclean,'" He had said. None of them had fully understood the words, but there was no mistaking the tone. There would be no compromise with the Pharisees on the washing of hands.

"Lord, Son of David, have mercy on me! My daughter is suffering terribly from demon possession." This woman was starting to annoy the apostles.

Therefore, it had brought a feeling of relief to cross the border into the region of Tyre and Sidon and enter the home of a Canaanite innkeeper. It was one thing to get arrested over an important matter like healing on the Sabbath, and quite another to put your life on the line for the right to eat with dirty hands.

But that was what was different with the Master. Whether the issue was great or small, He took on the Pharisees wherever He saw hypocrisy, even when compromise would have been easier. He treated people the same way. Lepers were equal to rabbis and tax collectors were on the same level as rulers of the synagogue in His eyes. The apostles had been rebuked on occasion for trying to decide who or what was important enough to deserve the attention of the Master.

So it surprised them that He was dismissing the appeals of this woman kneeling at his feet. *Why doesn't He just grant her wish and send her on so we can have some peace?* They argued about who should ask Him.

"Son of David, have mercy on me!" Again the words, and again no response from Jesus.

"Send her away," the one appointed by the Twelve pleaded. Now they waited to see if He would rebuke them or her.

Jesus looked first at the apostles gathered closely

around, then at the woman who was weeping at His feet.

She had run to the house where Jesus was staying when she had heard the rumor that several Jewish men had walked in from the south. A day earlier, travelers from the south had talked about the marvelous works being done in Gennesaret, just a few miles away. People were bringing their sick from all of the surrounding country and a rabbi was healing them, she had thought.

Perhaps He could help her daughter, she was told.

But even though it was less than a day's journey to Gennesaret, it was a lifetime away for the Canaanite woman. No rabbi would touch a Canaanite, particularly one that was demon possessed.

But when she had heard of the Jewish travelers in the town, she had run at once to the house. Perhaps He would be there, and perhaps He would show her mercy.

"Lord, Son of David, have mercy on me!" she said again. He fit the description. He must be the One. Her tears fell onto the floor as she wept uncontrollably. She could feel a hand on her shoulder. Looking up, she saw that it was He. She had never before seen eyes like those.

"Lord, help me!" she blurted out, never looking away from those eyes.

"First let the children eat all they want," He told her. "It is not right to take the children's bread and toss it to their dogs."

The apostles had never heard Jesus refuse to help someone before. Once a man asked Jesus, "If you can help," and Jesus had rebuked him, but even that man had been helped. Nor had they heard Him speak of anyone in the Jewish slang. The apostles still had some of their prejudices, and would often use words like "dog" to describe the non-Jews who wandered into the crowds, but only when they thought He wouldn't hear, because they knew He wouldn't approve. He even gave equal status to the children who got under their feet. So it was surprising to hear the rejection and doubly surprising to hear the slur they perceived in His reply.

But they hadn't heard what the Canaanite woman had heard, and they hadn't seen His eyes. Years as a social outcast because of her daughter's condition had made her accustomed to slurs, and this was not one. This was a test, she thought. The Rabbi had called her a "*kunaria*," a house pet. The Jews always called her people "*kuon*," the street dogs who ran in packs and ate the town's refuse. He had called her a "puppy" and He had said it with no judgment in those eyes. She would reply in kind.

"Yes, Lord, but even the dogs under the table eat the children's crumbs."

Then the eyes began to twinkle. She knew she had passed his test. He was smiling. "Woman, you have great faith. Your request is granted." She knelt at His feet once more and rose to run to her house.

As she left, the apostles began to realize the enormity of what Jesus had done. He had healed the daughter of a Canaanite, a woman of Tyre, and the word would surely reach the border before they did. If there was anything that would be less popular with the chief priests than healing Jews on the Sabbath, it would be healing "dogs" anytime.

Jesus indicated that it was time to start back. The crowds would come when they heard the story of the woman of faith. The refuge from the clamor they had sought would be gone. Yet there was no regret in the voice of the Master as He told them they must ready themselves to walk. He had chosen the first Gentile recipient of His power, and He had chosen well. She would tell others, and there would be some people of faith awaiting the apostles when they came this way again with news of His resurrection.

The apostles didn't know it now, but they would be outside the borders of Palestine many times in the future, much farther than the border towns of Tyre and Sidon. In fact, they would travel to the ends of the earth, proclaiming that in the eyes of the Lord all men and women have an equal place at His table.

Nathanael sits under a tree.

CHAPTER SEVEN

IT DOESN'T MATTER WHERE YOU'RE FROM IF YOU KNOW WHERE YOU'RE GOING

Prejudice. It literally means to "pre-judge." To make a decision without the facts.

It's particularly ugly when we do it based on outward factors: skin color, accent, appearances. Yet, in this story, that's exactly what Nathanael did. He prejudged the Teacher based on His hometown and not His teachings.

Of all of the prospects for the long-awaited Messiah, Jesus was an unlikely candidate. Born in a stable to parents not yet married. A "blue collar" worker. Not particularly handsome, the Scriptures say.

Perhaps those qualities were present (or absent) to trip up people like Nathanael. To his credit, however, Nathanael laid aside his prejudices, gave the Teacher a try, and devoted his life to Him.

When we decide to follow Jesus, we have to lay aside quite a few of our preconceived notions of Who He is and who we are, and that is what the story of Nathanael is all about.

Nathanael left the boat tired and hungry. The morning's fishing had been uneventful and shortly after noon the catch had been sold and the nets cleaned. There would be no more fishing until low tide that evening, so Nathanael had departed with his share of the profits, and headed in search of food and rest. It was about the ninth hour of the day, and he had been up since dawn, with only a small amount of dried fish to eat.

The life of a fisherman was demanding. The hours were long, the pay unsteady and the possibility of weather-related danger always present. But today, work had gone according to plan and now there were a few hours of rest ahead before the next shift.

After he had satisfied his hunger, Nathanael picked out a fig tree near his small home and sat underneath it. Pulling his head dressing down over his eyes, he slumped down to a comfortable position and breathed heavily.

He had moved to Bethsaida from Cana at the urging of his lifelong friend, Philip. Bethsaida was known for its fishing industry. In fact, the town's name meant "house of fishing." Nathanael took great pride in where he was from. If he was going to be a fisherman, he was going to live in the house of fishing. Only a resident for a few months, he no longer even admitted to coming from Cana.

Nathanael wondered, in the moments before he drifted off to sleep, where Philip might have been this morning. He was not at the boat at dawn, and the catch had been made without him. That wasn't like Philip to miss a day's work, and he was going to take it up with him later. But he was too tired right now to worry about that. As soon as he rested a while, he'd have time to check on Philip before evening.

He wasn't sure how long he had slept when he was awakened by a voice calling his name. It was Philip, running toward him gesturing quickly and talking rapidly. Perhaps he was groggy, or perhaps Philip wasn't making sense, but Nathanael was having trouble understanding what his friend was saying. Finally Philip reached him and drew a deep breath. Nathanael attempted to get in a quick question about where he had been during the morning run, but Philip shook his head and waved the question off. Trying to catch his breath, Philip blurted out his message.

"We have found the One Moses wrote about in the Law, and about Whom the prophets also wrote—Jesus of Nazareth, the son of Joseph," he said breathlessly.

Nathanael couldn't believe his ears. First, he had done the job of two men this morning. The owner of the boat had decided that since Nathanael was Philip's friend, he should perform both of their duties. Then, when he got a chance to rest from the double loads, he had been interrupted with a crazy story about finding the Promised One.

And where had he said this great One had come from? Nazareth? That tiny speck of a town? Birthplace of the Great Prophet?

Of all the things he wanted to bring up with Philip, for some reason Nathanael found himself starting with the Prophet story. He'd work his way back to the events of the morning, though he was becoming sure that Philip's absence and his announcement were somehow connected.

"Nazareth! Can anything good come from there?" Nathanael asked.

"Come and see," said Philip. And with that, he turned and walked toward the seashore, where Jesus had been teaching and calling out followers all day.

Nathanael hurried to catch Philip. There were still several things he wanted to discuss with him, beginning with his absence at the morning shift. But Philip was walking quickly, and Nathanael barely caught him before he heard the voice of Jesus calling out loudly, "Here is a true Israelite, in whom there is nothing false."

Nathanael stopped still. Was Jesus speaking to him? His first thought was to look around to see if He could be addressing anyone else. He cast a quick glance around to see if Jesus might have been talking to someone behind him. Philip observed this and laughed. Jesus had paid him a compliment, and he was uncertain whether he deserved it. Nathanael, however, pretended not to observe Philip and instead turned his attention to Jesus.

"How do You know me?" Nathanael asked.

Jesus answered, "I saw you while you were still under the fig tree before Philip called you."

Nathanael's jaw dropped perceptibly. How could He have known that he was napping a few minutes ago? Then his face began to turn red. If Jesus knew that, then He also knew that Nathanael had criticized His hometown. Should he apologize? Attempt to explain? Ignore it and hope that He hadn't heard? What about the fact that he had been sleeping in the middle of the day? Would he appear lazy to Jesus? Should he explain about the extra duty he had performed?

Although he couldn't decide what to do about these questions, he was sure that this was no ordinary man. "Rabbi, You are the Son of God; You are the King of Israel," he blurted out, bowing at Jesus' feet.

"You believe because I told you I saw you under the fig tree. You shall see greater things than that," Jesus said. He then added, "I tell you the truth, you shall see heaven open and the angels of God ascending and descending on the Son of Man."

Nathanael scrambled to his feet. He had already seen enough, yet Jesus promised that he would see more. As Jesus turned and continued along the shore, Nathanael took his place beside Philip and the others that He had called out earlier in the day.

As he walked, Nathanael had no way of knowing that he was headed to his hometown of Cana, where Jesus would perform His first miracle, one of many great things that Nathanael and the others were to witness in the days to come. He also had no way of knowing that he would never again have a hometown, as he left Bethsaida to follow the Man from Nazareth.

CHAPTER EIGHT

NOTHING AND EVERYTHING TO LOSE

On the first day of classes each fall, I look at my classroom of 60 freshmen away from home for the first time. They're scared, but the air of false bravado is so thick you can feel it in the air. Perhaps they're frightened of their new surroundings. Perhaps they've heard the upperclassmen's stories about their professors—stories carefully calculated to add to their fright.

As I look into about 120 eyes—eyes that could already use some extra sleep—the statistics from studies of youths reared in church-going homes haunt me. Even coming from some of the finest Christian homes imaginable, at least a third have already given up their virginity. Possibly five percent have been victims of emotional or sexual abuse at home, one or two may have been a victim of rape or date rape. Already, about ten percent or more have a problem with alcohol or drugs. Some may have had an abortion or have gotten a girlfriend pregnant.

They sit in class, carrying their individual secrets think-

*ing, "If they only knew, they wouldn't accept me." So they
stay silent, they seek no help, and the silence of their fellow
classmates only serves to keep the vicious cycle going. They
think: "I'm the only one who doesn't have it all together
here."*

*In this story, two individuals break the spiral of silence and
dare to come to Jesus in a public forum with their problems.
In a world where "I'm OK, You're OK" is both a bestselling
book and a cultural credo, their bravery stands as a reminder
that we can turn over our secret problems to the same Jesus
who has listened and healed for 2,000 years.*

The woman was in her mid-thirties, pale-skinned. In
fact, her skin was the chalky white color of one much
older than she. She looked at the magnitude of the
crowd and sighed. How could she ever get close to the
Master? And even if she got close, how could she sum-
mon the courage to tell Him her problem in front of all
the others? She had hoped that by getting to the shore
early in the morning she would be among the first to
welcome Jesus back from the area of the Gerasenes. Evi-
dently, many others had thought the same thing.

She was no more welcome in the crowd than a leper
would be. However, she had the advantage that her
problem was not so readily recognizable. If she
announced her problem, the Jewish crowd would probably scatter, for she was ceremonially unclean, and they
would be too, if they touched her. But she was far too
shy to take that route to the Master. She would just keep
her head lowered and work through the crowd, hoping
no one recognized her.

Twelve years ago she had noticed the problem. Her
period of menstruation had become erratic at first.
Then, it had become longer, until it seemed virtually to

never end. Today, the flow of blood was constant. This problem presented the woman with a multitude of problems: religious, medical, social and financial. Like being possessed by a demon, the disease had taken away her any hope of a normal life.

Jewish law decreed that any woman was ceremonially unclean during her period of menstruation for a period of seven days. But the law also provided for her problem as well, by declaring that any woman who had a discharge beyond her period would be unclean for the length of the bleeding plus seven days. Anyone touching her during that time would likewise be unclean.

She couldn't remember the last time her bleeding had stopped long enough to purchase the two doves and take them to the priest for the atonement sacrifice that made her ceremonially clean again. She had spent her entire savings on the treatments of doctors. Their treatments ranged from barbaric to trivial, as she tried baths, herbs, and other ritualistic cures without success.

The loss of blood left her with little energy and unable to work. She had never married. The disease had kept her from any type of normal social interaction in the Jewish community. She was now a pauper, with no income and no husband. She had heard of the Master and His ability to heal, and now she had summoned up the courage to brave the crowds and seek an audience with Him. It was her last resort.

Still unresolved in her mind was the problem of what to tell Jesus. Should she tell Him everything—the years of sickness, the embarrassment of being a social outcast, the poverty brought on by visiting doctors that had not helped? Would He touch her? Could He heal her without becoming unclean Himself?

She would worry about those problems later. Right now, her objective was to work through the crowds and get close to the Master.

On the other side of the crowd, Jairus was not having any problem approaching Jesus. The crowd parted in recognition of his position as a ruler of the synagogue. Few people of his stature even acknowledged Jesus, because of His claim to be the Son of God. Members of the crowd whispered and pointed as he walked between them, headed straight for Jesus. Jairus was aware of their stares and their whispers. He was also aware that he would have a price to pay in the socio-religious hierarchy for paying a visit to Jesus, but he was desperate. Jesus represented the last resort for his sick child, a twelve-year-old, his only daughter, now lying on her deathbed at home.

The ruler of the synagogue and the unclean woman edged their way closer to the Master from directions that were as different as were their stations in life. Jairus approached Jesus directly, his request ready. The woman approached Him from the rear, wondering what to say. Partners in desperation, neither realized they would reach the Master at the same time.

Carefully keeping her head down to avoid being recognized, the woman could tell by the tangle of humanity that she was getting close to Jesus. The crowd was thicker and the majority of those around her were the lame and blind seeking to be healed. She pressed deeper into the crushing crowd, and fell at Jesus' feet at the same moment as Jairus.

There they were: the ruler of the synagogue and the woman who hadn't been clean enough to worship for months. The one who had been ushered through the crowd, and the one who had feared being recognized. They were virtually face to face at the feet of the One who would treat them the same. She had nothing left to lose; he would pay any price.

She recognized Jairus, but he did not know her. His presence compounded her problem. How could she speak of her unclean state in the presence of a ruler of the synagogue? Men such as he could banish her from the crowd. Had she made her way to the Master only to be the victim of bad timing? As she pondered her situation, Jairus spoke first.

"My little daughter is dying. Please come and put Your hands on her that she will be healed and live." Looking down, Jesus had compassion on him. As He turned to go with Jairus, He had not yet acknowledged the woman who had also fallen at His feet. The crowd was so thick that she had gone unnoticed.

Her chance to speak to Jesus was fading fast. Her mind raced. Something inside her said to reach out to Him. Even touching His clothing would do. She must do it quickly. Jesus was leaving and the crowd was closing in behind Him. In a lunge of desperation and faith, she touched just the hem of His garment. Immediately she sensed that her bleeding stopped. Her plan had worked!

Sensing that power had gone out from Him, Jesus stopped and turned. "Who touched My clothes?"

The woman froze and cowered in fear. She hadn't anticipated this. Surely the crowd was thick enough that she could stay still. She waited and listened while some of the Twelve attempted to tell Jesus that with so many people around Him that it would be impossible to isolate one person who had touched Him. She hoped He would listen to them. But Jesus would not be put off by His apostles. He continued to look for the one who had touched His clothing.

She was quivering now. What if she had to come forward and give an explanation for her action? The crowd would scatter, and some might even throw stones at her. All those who had touched her would have to wash their clothes, bathe and wait until evening before becoming ceremonially clean again. In their anger at the prospect of this ritualistic inconvenience, they might harm her.

Still, she knew that she had been healed. And the One with the power to heal a twelve-year-old disease would also have the power to ascertain who had touched Him. Better that she admit it now than wait and face His wrath as well as the crowd's.

She came forward and fell once again at Jesus' feet. When He touched her and helped her to her feet, it was the first time another human had intentionally touched her in months. The feel of that touch gave her courage, and she stood to speak. In the presence of the crowd she told her story. As she spoke, she noticed that the crowd backed up a little, giving her more room than before. She told of her twelve years of suffering and of her plan to touch His clothing and of her instantaneous healing.

Reaching out to her, Jesus said, "Daughter, your faith has healed you." Looking out at the crowd, who were still wary of her, Jesus added with a loud voice, "Go in peace, and be healed from your suffering."

In one act, Jesus had stopped both the suffering and the isolation that came with it. She had been restored to her health and to her community. She could once again know the joy of normal life. She could be accepted into her former social circle again.

As Jesus walked away, Jairus was at His side. His daughter, though now dead, would be raised. But because of his association with the One who claimed to be the Son of God, Jairus would lose his stature as ruler of the synagogue. He would pay the same price that the woman had paid for the past twelve years—isolation and financial reversal—but his faith would be rewarded each time he looked into his daughter's eyes.

A young man begins his journey to
meet Jesus on the other side of the lake.

Chapter Nine

Counting the Cost

Why is it that we find it so easy to pour ourselves out for others—our children, our parents, our bosses—and so hard to sacrifice for the One who gave it all up for us? In the story below, a young man has to come to grips with that question. For years a dutiful son, in one moment he was forced to make a decision to drop his worldly obligations and follow Christ or return to his life of routine.

Perhaps, like Martha busying herself in the kitchen while Christ taught in the parlor, we confuse our many activities with pleasing God. Our committee meetings, impending deadlines and numerous good works become a placebo for the strong medicine that few want to taste—the demand for total sacrifice.

The decision the young man faced on that fateful day 2,000 years ago will face each of us, too. To choose life is to leave some things behind for dead, something Paul acknowledged in his letter to the Galatians. And what we are forced to leave behind may be as startling as the dead father that Jesus told this young man to leave. We might actually have to leave behind a calendar full of church business (and busyness) to sit at the Master's feet.

The encounter between Jesus and the young man was brief and without pressure, lasting only two verses in Matthew's account. And so it is with us. Jesus knocks but he doesn't pound. There's no record in the scriptures of how the young man responded. Here is one possible scenario.

His father had died the previous day. For weeks, the physicians had tended to him daily, but finally there was nothing more that could be done.

Through his father's illness, the son had been there. He had kept the family business of tanning skins going, working twice as hard to make up for the absence of his father, and forsaking his own career dreams. At night, he would read to him from the writings of Moses, or go over the ledgers of the family business with him. As his father grew weaker, he would simply hold his hand, bathe his forehead, and sing softly to him in the room's dim light.

And even now that his father was gone, there was more to do. By custom, he was to be buried on the third day after death, following an appropriate period of mourning. But the mourning would have to wait. Today, he had to buy a plot for burial, obtain a shroud, and hire someone to prepare the body with spices and wrappings. Tomorrow there would be more.

As funerals went, it would be modest. Yet even a modest burial involved countless details. The son knew that his mother could not make such arrangements herself. His only sister lived in Galilee and probably wouldn't make it to the funeral, just like she hadn't made it to visit during the illness. She had a family of her own, and responsibilities there, and messages from her were few. There were two additional sons in the family at one time, but one had died as a boy years ago, and the other, the oldest son, had become estranged from his father years ago when they shared the family business. He was not even expected to come to the funeral. So all arrangements had fallen to the one son who had remained at home for more than 25 years.

He would have liked to have left, but by the time he became a man, his father's health was failing and the tanning process was hard on him. His father could not continue to work without his son's participation in the business, so he had postponed his dreams of being a merchant. He had planned to travel to lands in the East he had heard about in search of exotic spices and foods unavailable in Judea. Even now, his father's death did not free him to pursue his dream, since he must care for his mother, and the life of the road offered no assurances of safety or profit.

But the exotic lands to the East were far from his mind today as he walked the streets of Capernaum. There were arrangements to be handled and purchases to be made so that his father could have a proper Jewish burial. Even in death, his father's needs came above his own.

As he walked through the city's business district, he found few businesses open. Most were closed for the day—strange for this thriving seaport. A few blocks further he heard a commotion. Perhaps this crowd was the reason why all the shops were closed. Curious, he walked to where the crowd had gathered and inquired of one of the men what had brought him there.

"It's the one they call Jesus," the man said excitedly. "He's been here all morning, and He's cured a man of leprosy, raised a Roman centurion's slave from the dead and healed a woman of a fever. He also cast out demons from some."

"Did you see all this?" asked the son.

"Most of it, though he's gone inside some of the houses of the sick, and he told the centurion that his servant would be healed by the time he got home."

"And you believe that?" the son asked.

"I do," the man said. "And if you had seen all we saw today, you would believe it too."

Just then, the one he had called Jesus began to speak. The son stopped his worrying about funeral preparations long enough to listen. He spoke simply, using illustrations to make his points. He spoke of wide and narrow gates and compared them to the route to eternal life. He spoke of good and bad trees being recognized by their fruit. He told a story about a wise builder and foolish builder who each built a house, yet only one withstood the storm.

As He spoke, the son thought Jesus was talking directly to him. Hadn't he spent his life on the narrow road? Hadn't he borne good fruit, laid a good foundation? Maybe it was time for something bold. Maybe he should follow this Teacher named Jesus, as many in the crowd seemed to be doing. He found himself edging closer to the front of the crowd.

As he approached Jesus, he heard one man say, "Teacher, I will follow you wherever you go."

Jesus replied, "Foxes have holes and birds have nests, but the Son of Man has no place to lay His head." The thought of living without permanent shelter must have frightened the man who spoke up, because he became silent and let the crowd come between him and Jesus.

That possibility, however, didn't trouble the son, who had long dreamed of the romance of life on the road. If it couldn't be as a trader, perhaps it could be as one of the followers of this itinerant teacher. He decided that it was time to speak. He really wanted to go with this Jesus and watch these miracles for himself and listen to more teachings.

Summoning his courage, he spoke. "Lord, I will follow you wherever you go. Only, first let me go and bury my father."

Turning to the son and looking directly at him, Jesus replied, "Follow Me, and let the dead bury their own dead."

As Jesus turned His attention to the next petitioner, His words burned like a brand on the conscience of the son. "Let the dead bury their own dead," He had said. What had that meant, he wondered?

Perhaps Jesus's command referred to his brother, who had been dead to his father for years. His brother was a bad tree, producing bad fruit. He had no problem leaving him behind. He was pretty sure the command also referred to his sister. He could leave her behind, and force her to own up to some of her responsibilities as a daughter.

But what would happen to his mother? The question gnawed at him as Jesus began to get into a boat with his closest friends. Many were talking of making the journey around the water to the other side, even though it would take all night. The son wanted to go with them, yet he worried about his mother. He would double her anguish if he failed to return home that evening from his duties.

The Teacher's boat was sailing into the distance now, and the crowd had dispersed to go back to their homes. Most of the talk of following the teacher to the other side had been just talk, and few appeared prepared to make the trip. Most were content with going home and telling the stories of what they had seen and heard to those who were not there. For them, the day had been more of a carnival than a religious experience.

But the son wanted so much more than that. For in those few simple illustrations he had seen the story of his life: the son who walked a straight path. But right now, he felt as if his narrow path led to nowhere. Yet, he sensed that in the words of the Teacher, he could find direction.

However, if he left his mother now, he would be worse than his brother in the eyes of the Jews. So he stood by the dock with his problem. Outside, he was the family's solid oak, while inside, he felt like a tree that had lived its life in the stifling shadow of his father, with no roots of his own, and certainly no fruit. He was simply surviving, not thriving. It was finally time to bear fruit, he thought.

As he watched the boat disappear into the twilight's

shadows, he determined two things. First, his mother would understand when she got word of his decision. Second, the boat's direction would take it across the Sea of Galilee into the region of the Gadarenes by morning and he could be there when it arrived if he walked all night.

CHAPTER TEN

COME FORWARD AND BE COUNTED

In a county near my home recently, there was a tie vote in an election. A recount was held, and then another. The final verdict: the two candidates had tied. There would have to be another election.

Everyone's vote had counted. Not one person had wasted their effort in going to the polls, for if they had not gone, the other side would have won. And think of the many potential voters who mentally kicked themselves for not taking a little time to do such a small thing as voting.

It's easy to overlook the small things. I stood one day with the gawkers as a truck ran off the road and plowed through a home down the street from my home. My wife made lemonade and took it to the family and to the friends who were feverishly trying to board up the damage before nightfall.

I thought it peculiar that someone who had just lost half of their house would need such a small thing as lemonade. My wife thought it peculiar that someone would look at such tragedy and do nothing. She was right.

Jesus could have fed the crowd in the story below in any manner He wished. God had rained manna from heaven for decades and kept His people alive. I think, however, that He used the little boy's lunch to impress upon His apostles how far a little gesture could go.

He later said that even a cup of water offered in His name was worthy of reward. I'm sure He smiled on the lemonade as well.

The boy had never seen such a crowd. He heard someone say that there must be at least 5,000 men present—a common Jewish way of counting crowds. Odd, he thought. Why not count everybody equally? He knew, however, it was not his place to ask.

He was simply content on this day to be one of the crowd, one of the great uncounted among the women and children. He had just turned ten years old, and soon he would be a man in the eyes of the law. This morning, his mother had made him a lunch and allowed him to follow the crowd to hear the Teacher. It was his first trip alone, and he was feeling quite a bit like a man, even if he wasn't counted among them.

When he left Bethsaida that morning, he received his instructions from his mother. Stay with the crowd. Eat all your lunch. Get back before dark. His mother was happy to have him go because she had heard so much good about the Teacher. She would have gone herself, but she had smaller children who couldn't make the trip to the countryside. The boy's father showed little interest in the Teacher, saying only that others had come before and others would follow. Besides, he had to go sell his goods at the temple for the day's sacrifices.

As he walked out to hear the Teacher, the boy couldn't have known that he would stand out from the crowd that day. At times, he used his small size to get close to the Teacher, but as soon as he wriggled in close, the grown-ups always seemed to get in front of him. He also had to constantly give ground to those carrying the lame and leading the blind up to the Teacher for healing.

He noticed that the Teacher was accompanied by several men who constantly tried to keep Him moving, holding the crowd away. At one point, the Teacher seemed to scold them for preventing children from getting close to Him. This made the boy happy: the Teacher liked children. If he could just get close to Him, perhaps he would get to touch Him.

By mid-afternoon, the boy remembered the food in his pouch. His mother had packed five small, hard barley loaves, a stout bread that lasted weeks after baking. In addition, he had two small fish, preserved by drying and salting. It was a typical meal for traveling, and was more efficient than tasty, but he wasn't complaining. No one around him seemed to have as much as he. First, however, he had to refill his sheepskin with water, for this type of meal was not made for a dry mouth on a hot day.

Just then, the crowd movement stopped while the Teacher's advisors conferred. They seemed to be arguing among themselves. Then the word went out: whoever has food, bring it to the Teacher. The boy hesitated. Didn't his mother tell him to eat all his lunch? But the Teacher must be hungry and needed it more. Wouldn't his mother approve of giving it to the Teacher? On the other hand, the Teacher could have His choice of anyone's lunch. Surely He wouldn't settle for dry bread and preserved fish.

He decided to wait to offer his lunch to the Teacher after others had taken theirs. That way, the Teacher could see that his was nothing special, and he would be able to obey both his mother and the command to produce his food. That was it: obey the order, but just don't be the first. He'd wait, get in the line as it formed, show his lunch and be done with it.

But a strange thing happened. No one stepped forward. There was no food in the entire crowd! The boy gulped, realizing that he couldn't hide in a long line. He must go up alone. He didn't mind the Teacher eating his lunch; he just didn't want to take it up in front of all those people and hand it to one of those men who had been rebuking children earlier. Besides, it was the lunch of a poor boy, not a meal for the Teacher. Still, the order had gone out: bring your food to the Teacher.

Slowly, the boy approached one of the Teacher's men named Andrew. He held out the sack and apologized for its contents. "It's not much, and it's a little dry. But if you want it, it's yours," he said.

Andrew took both the boy and his lunch to the Teacher, where he repeated his apology and his offer. The Teacher reached down, smiled and patted the boy and took the lunch. Holding the pouch up to the sky, the Teacher gave thanks for the food and instructed the entire crowd to be seated. He then ordered Andrew and the rest to pass the food among the crowd. It was at that moment that the boy realized that his lunch was not for the Teacher. It was for everyone!

How could that be possible? I could eat that entire lunch by myself, he thought.

But as the helpers passed through the crowd, first with the bread and then with the fishes, *the supply never ran out.* The loaves and the fishes multiplied as long as anyone continued to want them.

And when the meal was over, *the leftover portions were greater than what the boy had brought!* Then Andrew returned his pouch, with as much food as he had originally offered the Teacher.

The boy asked Andrew how it was possible to feed so many from so little. Andrew smiled and explained that with the Master, anything was possible. Andrew explained that the boy saw with the eyes of logic, while Jesus taught His followers to see with the eyes of faith. With that, he returned to where the Teacher was healing the sick.

The boy pondered the statement. Though he didn't understand it fully, he stored it in his heart. What he thought it meant was that one who hadn't even counted in the estimate of the crowd size had made the most important contribution.

The paralytic at the pool.

Chapter Eleven

Maybe Today Will Be the Day

Have you ever wanted something badly and when you got it you didn't know what to do with it? Or maybe it turned out to be a mixed blessing? Did you begin to wonder why you had wanted it so badly in the first place?

The Scriptures record an incident of a lame man who wanted so badly to walk that he spent most of his life beside a pool alleged to have healing powers. Yet after a lifetime of waiting for the power to walk, his healing created a political problem and a personal crisis. As a lame man he had no enemies, and at least a few friends who would help him to the pool. As a whole man, he was made a pawn in a struggle between Jesus and those who would seek to kill Him.

Perhaps the highs and lows of life come close together for a reason. It makes sense, if you stop to think about it. It returns us to a dependence on God.

The Romans had a tradition of honoring returning war heroes with a parade. While the general rode the chariot through the cheering throngs, a servant stood by his side and whispered in his ears, "Remember, thou art only a man."

The lesson was clear: "Don't confuse military prowess with omniscience."

In the story below, the message was like that to the Roman general: "Don't confuse the ability to walk with being on the right path."

While the lame man probably would have preferred to have spent days enjoying his new-found ability to walk, Jesus brought him back down quickly to a realization that he was not yet whole. He still had to confront his spiritual sickness as well. Perhaps that's the message to us the next time our highs and lows seem to blur together. He's still working on us, too.

Maybe today will be the day, he thought to himself. The crowd around the pool at the Sheep's Gate wasn't too large yet, and most of them were at least as crippled as he was, many of them more so.

He quickly scanned the crowd, noting the regulars, who like himself waited for that one chance to be healed. He took note that no one yet seemed to have any help. That was good. Maybe today would be the day.

No one really knew why the pool's waters worked like they did. For as long as anyone could remember, one person was healed each time the waters moved. No one knew how it happened or when it would happen, yet it always seemed to work. But always for someone else. In thirty-eight years, he had seen a lot of them come and go. The blind usually got healed the fastest. They simply waited until they heard the commotion with their keen ears. They would feel their way quickly down the steps and immerse themselves into the healing waters before others could respond to the noise.

Those that had withered hands but strong legs were also healed within weeks, leaving the paralyzed at the bottom of the survival chain, unable to reach the waters.

If only he had some help. He had seen others helped into the waters by others patient enough to wait for the miraculous stirring. On occasion, he had even talked someone into waiting and watching with him. But inevitably hours gave way to days and he lost his help. . . and his chance. Someone else always got his miracle.

His life for nearly four decades had been one of "what if's." What if the water healed all who plunged in? What if the pool were not so deep in the ground, so that a paralyzed person could simply roll into the pool without fear of death? What if there were a system of justice where each waited his turn and healing came to all in the order of their arrival at the pool? What if just one friend came and stayed until the waters moved, no matter how long it took?

But day after day justice never prevailed, friends never came, and the waters healed only the swiftest and least deserving. But as he thanked those who laid him beside the pool, he said today, as he did almost every day, "Maybe today will be the day." In fact, he was so positive that his chances were good, he ordered his carriers not to leave him propped up by one of the five covered colonnades, but to place him directly beside the steps leading down to the pool. Behind his back, they rolled their eyes at his request. He was only going to get burned by the sun, and besides, it had been days since the last disturbance of the waters. Some said that the waters had lost their power permanently.

But thirty-eight years of experience told the paralytic that the power always came back. And today he was optimistic. No one there was healthier than he, no one there had helpers and the crowds were low because of the expected heat and the great number of days since the last miracle. Maybe today would be the day.

Just then a number of people entered the pool area. This can't be good, he thought. They're here to help someone. Worse than that, some otherwise healthy person might jump in the waters to heal a boil. Somebody is going to steal my miracle, he thought.

He watched as he saw one of them, a man about thirty years old, talk to some of the others who were crippled. They, in turn, pointed to him, and sent the man walking to him. Silently he vowed not to reveal any information about the pool to this fellow. He obviously had a sick relative somewhere and was looking for information about the pool. As the pool's longest resident he was the usual source of information about the waters, but not today. The conditions were just too right to lose out to someone less deserving than he.

"Do you want to get well?"

The stranger's question shocked the paralytic man. No one had ever asked him that question in thirty-eight years. Didn't his perseverance speak for itself? Still, there was something in the stranger's voice that was sincere, and besides, He might stay and help. He decided to make his best case and see if the stranger would stay, at least for a few hours. Things were beginning to look up, he told himself.

"Sir," he started. Although he was older than the stranger, anyone who was walking erect commanded respect from the paralytic, so he addressed all men as "sir."

"I have no one to help me into the pool when the water is stirred. While I am trying to get in, someone else goes down ahead of me."

Having said this, the paralytic paused. Perhaps he should share with Him his secret feeling that the waters were long overdue. But could he trust Him with that special information? He might still be gathering information for a sick relative. He might be one of those perfectly healthy people who from time to time jumped into the waters first in hopes of finding a fountain of youth or even an aphrodisiac—two of the legends that had cropped up about the pool over the years. The very thought of those types made him ill. What if this stranger was one of those? Better to remain quiet now, he thought.

"Get up! Pick up your mat and walk."

The words rang inside the paralytic's head. At first he wanted to laugh, but the words had been spoken with such authority they commanded at least some respect. But Who was this Man who could just command paralyzed men to walk?

All eyes were on him now. Most of the regulars had known him for years. He saw in their eyes eagerness and anticipation, for if he could be healed without the waters, so could they. They actually wanted him to try it! Let them fall on their faces, he thought.

Just then, he felt a strange sensation—he could feel

his lower limbs! It was a strangely familiar feeling, yet one that he had not felt for a long time. Slowly, with the unsteadiness of a toddler, he rose. What should he do next? Hadn't the stranger said something about his mat? He remembered that he was supposed to pick it up and start walking. He would rather leave the ragged old thing there, he thought, but this was no time to make the stranger mad.

As he knelt down to roll up the mat, the former paralytic wondered if this was some kind of cruel hoax. Would he be able to get up when he had finished with his mat? He hurried with his task and rose again, relieved that he was able to do it a second time. He had so much to do, so many people to go tell, and even a few scores to settle with people who hadn't needed the pool but had climbed in anyway.

As he was muttering his thanks and secretly hoping to get away from the presence of anyone with so much power, he heard a question directed at him by the Pharisees who had come running at the sound of commotion. "It is the Sabbath; the Law forbids you to carry your mat."

Great, he thought to himself. On his legs less than a minute and problems already. The mat meant nothing to him; he could surely leave it. Yet the stranger had specifically said to take it, and He was certainly not One to be angered.

"The Man who made me well said to me 'Pick up your mat and walk,'" the former paralytic explained, hoping that the Pharisees would direct their inquisition elsewhere and let him get out of the Sheep's Gate area before the stranger changed His mind. In thirty-eight years he had never seen a miracle like this one, and the didn't want any trouble to ruin it.

"Who is this fellow who told you to pick it up and walk?" the Pharisees asked. As the healed man turned to show them his benefactor, he discovered that the stranger had slipped through the crowd and left. Since he could no longer anger his healer, he dropped the mat and fled from the Pharisees, his feet still unaccustomed to the normal routines of walking or running.

When he was sure that he was free of the Pharisees, he began to search for the stranger. Questions ran through his mind. He had anticipated that today would be the day, but he had thought the miracle would come in the conventional way—not from the hand of a man. He saw a crowd gathered at the temple and went to see if possibly the stranger was there. He moved easily through the crowd, since no one noticed him from the pool. All paralytics look alike to the healthy, he thought. Sure enough, at the center of the crowd was the stranger. As he rehearsed what he wanted to say to the stranger, he was surprised that the Man, whom others were calling Jesus, singled him out of the crowd and motioned for him to draw near. When he did, Jesus said to him, "See, you are well again. Stop sinning or something worse will happen to you."

How did Jesus know the origin of his injury? For years, he had passed off the condition as a birth defect. But Jesus knew, and He had healed him anyway. Now Jesus was as concerned about his moral well-being as He had been about his physical body. And the healed man knew what he must do.

With boldness, he hurried back to the Pharisees. He wanted no trouble, especially since the one called Jesus obviously knew his past. But he felt compelled to proclaim the name of Jesus and there was no better place to begin than with those who had asked.

"It was Jesus. Jesus made me well," he blurted out when he reached the Pharisees still conferring by the pool. They had suspected the answer, and sternly commanded that he not tell anyone else. The healed man listened to their warnings, looked at his newly-perfect feet and thought for a moment. Then slowly, in a calculated move to show his allegiance, he picked up his mat, rolled it in front of them, defiantly hoisted it over his shoulder and walked away to join the Master of the Sabbath.

CHAPTER TWELVE

The King Pays His Taxes

*If you were king for a day, under what rules would you
live? Which rules would you ignore if you had the power to do
so? To whom would you listen, and whom would you ignore?*

*In this story, the apostles get an object lesson from Jesus as
the same Master who overturned the sellers' tables in the temple paid the lowliest of taxes to avoid offending the Jews.*

It was the season of the temple tax again, and the tax
collector of Capernaum listened in interest to the offer
being made to him. Catch the Teacher in a tax problem,
they said, and we'll double your collections for the year.

The tax dated back to Mosaic times. The half-shekel
required by law amounted to about two days wages per
man, and all men were required to pay the tax during
the month of Adar, in the spring.

The temple tax helped to pay for the sacrifices offered on behalf of the entire nation—an unblemished year-old lamb in the morning and in the evening, plus oil, wine and flour offerings. The tax also paid for the expensive priestly vestments and other temple expenses.

Unlike the Roman taxes, the temple taxes were not hated. They were collected from the Jews by fellow Jews, and all of the monies collected stayed within the Jewish community. Yet, still they were taxes, and sometimes it was an effort to get every name on the book to pay before the required date in the middle of the month, and the rewards for all the effort were quite low.

That is why the offer had intrigued the temple tax collector of Capernaum. Here was a chance to actually see a financial reward from the collection of the small temple tax. For years, he watched with envy as the ones who collected the Roman taxes got rich off their commission, yet he was still hardly more than a ward of the temple. And it stung him to know that the Roman tax collectors held him in contempt for the lowly position he filled.

He had not known the men who had come to him with the offer, and he was sure that the less he knew, the better. But he did know opportunity when he heard it, and he had quickly agreed.

When the Teacher arrived in Capernaum, however, the crowds were great. The tax collector could not get near enough to Him to ask Him for the tax. He watched from a distance, waiting his chance and feeling his reward slip away.

The Pharisees who chose him waited too, observing

the scene from a different angle. To them, the tax represented the best opportunity to trap the Teacher. He observed few of the temple laws. He had healed on the Sabbath on numerous occasions. But those healings had struck such awe in the crowds that to arrest Him on those occasions would have been folly.

Yes, it would be the half-shekel tax that would do it. If He refused to pay, as they suspected, He would no longer be a sympathetic figure to the crowds who had just been levied themselves. So the Pharisees watched from the edge of the crowd, looking first at the Teacher, then at their pathetic cohort, nervously shifting his weight from foot to foot while awaiting his opening.

Unaware that he was being watched by his "employers," the tax collector stood impatiently looking for an opening that never came. Finally, he decided to talk to the one who had come in with the Teacher. He was standing off to the side while the masses crowded around Jesus. Maybe he could get to Him through this one. He moved towards Peter.

The Pharisees watched in horror as he approached one of the apostles. They wanted a direct confrontation with Jesus in front of witnesses. Now this fool was going to upset the whole plot. The apostle would pay and the chance would be gone. It wasn't the half-shekel they wanted. It was the Teacher.

"Doesn't your teacher pay the temple tax?" he asked, holding out his hand, palm up. The Pharisees gnashed their teeth in disgust. They hadn't heard the question from a distance, but they could tell by the gesture that they had missed their opportunity. The job had required prudence beyond the ability of this fellow. They began to walk away.

Peter ignored the hand and considered the question. What impertinence! Didn't he know that Jesus could tear down this temple and rebuild it within three days? He was not beholden to any man for any amount of money, Peter thought. Better to tell this man what he wants to hear than to debate him, though.

Still ignoring the hand, Peter replied, "Yes, He does," and walked away without offering to pay, and with only a hint of remorse at the misleading answer. In truth, he had never seen the Teacher pay, but what did it matter? It was only a half-shekel.

As Peter walked one way and the Pharisees another, the tax collector saw this chance at a bounty walk away with them. And Jesus, from His vantage point saw it all.

Within the hour, the apostles had made their way into a follower's home. Peter was about to recount the episode for Jesus, when Jesus turned to him with a question instead.

"What do you think, Simon? From whom do the kings of earth collect duty and taxes—from their own sons or from others?"

Peter almost choked at the question. Jesus had knowledge of his encounter with the tax collector! Would he be rebuked again by Jesus?

He had feared that he said the wrong thing to the tax collector. It hadn't been a lie, just an answer of convenience. He just didn't want to be drawn into a lengthy debate with someone so low as a temple tax collector. Matthew had once told the apostles the joke about them in the profession: they weren't smart enough to be crooked. After all, what was a half-shekel? But now, here he was, once again, answering to Jesus for another rash decision.

"From others," he answered softly, not looking at Jesus.

"Then the sons are exempt," Jesus said.

He knew it! That's what he had almost said to the tax collector. That Jesus, the Son of God, owed no taxes to run His Father's house. That's what he should have said. But his pride had gotten in the way. The tax collector hadn't seemed worthy of a theological discussion.

Jesus continued: "But so that we may not offend them, go to the lake and throw out your line. Take the first fish you catch; open its mouth and you will find a shekel. Take it and give it to them for my tax and yours."

The words stung. Peter would have to go looking for the temple tax collector to pay the smallest of all taxes, and he would have to go fishing to get the coin. He could just imagine the expression of the tax collector now. He would know Peter had lied. And he would know that he had been rebuked.

As Peter left, he was not sure if he would find a literal coin in the mouth of a fish, or if he would catch enough fish to sell and pay the temple tax for both of them. He often confused the times when Jesus spoke literally with the times He spoke allegorically. But he was sure of this: the One who was both God and Man hadn't judged the worth of the tax by the status of the collector. He mulled over that thought as he walked towards the water.

The blind man by the road.

Chapter Thirteen

Too Blind to See the Light

Snap judgments. We all make them. Easy answers. We all want them. Snap judgments and easy answers function as a sort of mental shorthand that helps us bypass deep thinking.

For instance, none of us likes to wrestle with the problem of why a just God allows injustice to reign in the world. Most certainly Habakkuk didn't when he challenged God's choice of the severely wicked Chaldeans to punish the merely wicked Jewish nation.

Neither do we like to wrestle with the question of why a compassionate God would allow disease and death in the world.

The Jews solved this dilemma by developing a simple calculus: bad things happened to bad people, while good things happened to good people. It was an easy theology built on snap judgments. Where there was pain, there was sin; where there was prosperity, there was righteousness.

As transparent as this theology was, even the apostles held it—as we will see in this story—and remnants of it remain today. Jesus, however, dispels that notion in this story and sets an example for us to do the same.

The blind man heard the group approaching and prepared to hold out his bowl. His blindness had heightened his sense of hearing, and he could tell that this was a large group approaching. They were walking with the heavy set shuffling of travelers. Then he heard the question.

"Rabbi, who sinned, this man or his parents that he was born blind?"

The words stung. Did the speaker think that a blind man had no ears? Or feelings? It had been like this his entire life. In the Jewish culture a handicapped person bore a double burden. First was the handicap. Second was the traditional belief that the handicap was the punishment of God for earlier sins.

Even the apostles held this view, and it was one of them who had addressed the question to Jesus.

The blind man was about to voice his indignation at the impertinent question when he heard the answer.

"Neither this man nor his parents sinned," said Jesus, "but this happened so that the work of God might be displayed in his life. As long as it is day, we must do the work of Him who sent Me. Night is coming when, no one can work. While I am in the world, I am the light of the world."

The blind man heard the words, but he only understood the first part about his blindness not being a result of sin. The rest confused him. Especially the part about night coming. Though he was blind, he knew that it was still before midday. Someone would bring him a meal then and take his morning gifts away for safe keeping. Since they had not yet come, and since he was not yet hungry, he assumed it was only mid-morning.

As he was pondering what the speaker had said, the blind man had no way of seeing what He was now doing. Jesus knelt to the ground and spit on the dirt, making a small ball of mud with His saliva. The blind man jumped back slightly. He had heard the sound of spitting before, and it was usually aimed at him by those who felt more powerful by harming the weak.

Walking up to the blind man, Jesus put a small amount of the mud on each of his eyes. The mud stung and made his blind eyes water. He immediately sputtered a protest of oaths and threats that he, of course, could never carry out.

He was accustomed to occasional trouble with robbers, but no one was low enough to assault a blind person. But his state of confusion was greater than his pain. One minute he had been trying to figure out what the speaker meant by calling Himself the light of the world, and the next, someone had put something in his eyes that felt like the sand that occasionally blew in them.

Just then the One that had put something in his eyes spoke. "Go wash in the pool of Siloam," He said. With that, the speaker walked off toward the town gate as the blind man sputtered in pain and in protest. There was no one to hear his cries, however, and the suggestion of the pool sounded like a good one, so the blind man turned and walked in the direction of the pool outside the city.

He had walked the path to the pool before. It was easy to find, since he could follow the voices of happy children who enjoyed splashing in the water. Today, however, was the Sabbath, a fact that he remembered as he failed to hear the familiar noises. This would make it harder to find the pool. No one was out walking the streets who might see him and help.

Frustration began to set in as the blind man mulled over the events of the past few minutes. First someone had made fun of his condition. Then someone else had defended him, using phrases he didn't understand. One person had called the speaker Rabbi; another had called Him Jesus. It was the Rabbi who had put something in his eyes. He was certain of that.

He only remembered a little of the rest of the conversation. Hadn't the Rabbi said something about the work of God being displayed in his life? The blind man wondered what He had meant by that. He also wondered when would he reach the pool to get this burning to stop. One thing he knew for sure: whenever he reached the authorities, he was going to report this Rabbi called Jesus for what He had done.

Eventually, he made it to the pool, with the help of a Samaritan traveler who was going there to water his animals. He washed the stinging mud out of his eyes and blinked. To his astonishment, the stinging of the mud was replaced by the burning of the light he now saw. The light from the sun was bright, and he immediately fell to his knees, weak from the shock of his first glimpse of life. The Samaritan hurried over to help him to his feet and decided to take him home. The blind man had been in the sun too long, he thought. He was weak in the legs and muttering something about being able to see. The Samaritan lifted him onto his donkey and asked him where he lived.

By the time he got home, the blind man had tested his eyes several times. At first he would open them only for a second, then longer, until he began to keep them open for short periods of time. He dismounted the donkey like a new child just beginning to walk, his balance affected by his new ability to see. Finding it easier to shut his eyes and walk as he formerly did, he thanked the Samaritan and entered his home with his eyes tightly shut.

Over the next few hours, he practiced his eyesight in the dimness of his familiar home. When he became confident that he could walk unaided, he ventured outside to tell his neighbors the news. Since it was the Sabbath, most of them were in their houses. Almost immediately a crowd gathered around the man as several shouted the news from house to house. A debate arose among them about whether this was the same beggar they had lived around for years. Some said he was; others said it was only someone who looked like him. Few had ever bothered to look at his face as he walked stooped with a cane down the narrow streets. Now that he was standing erect and looking at them squarely, it was hard to believe he was the same man.

"I am the man," he kept insisting to the doubters.

"How then were your eyes opened?" they demanded.

He replied, "The man they call Jesus made some mud and put it on my eyes. He told me to go to Siloam and wash. So I went and washed, and then I could see."

"Where is this man?" they asked him. "I don't know," he said.

Someone from the street had run to the temple and told the leaders of the Pharisees what was happening in the street. Fearing that it was yet another miracle by the One who claimed to get His powers from God, they summoned the formerly blind man to the temple.

When he arrived, the Pharisees asked him to tell the story once more.

"He put mud on my eyes," the man replied, "and I washed and now I see."

Huddling together, the Pharisees argued about the man's story. "This man is not from God for He does not keep the Sabbath," some said. "How can a sinner do such miraculous signs?" Others asked of the skeptics. As the Pharisees proceeded to argue heatedly among themselves, the healed man thought to himself that he had heard it all before: good people do good works and have perfect bodies. When someone doesn't fit the traditional wisdom, they are labeled a sinner. This Jesus must be a lot like him, he thought. Always getting criticized unfairly.

As he was thinking about this, he heard them address him once again.

"What have you to say about Him? It was your eyes He opened."

The man replied, "He is a prophet." It was a safe answer, he thought. His only desire at this point was to get away from this inquisition.

However, one of the Pharisees had left the temple to get the man's parents. The Pharisees wished to question them in hopes of finding a way to explain away the miracle. They arrived, frightened and bewildered at being ordered away from a quiet Sabbath, and saw their son in the middle of the crowd, looking different than when they had seen him a few days before.

The healed man didn't recognize the couple as he wasn't aware of the plan to go find his parents. He looked up as the Pharisees asked the question, "Is this your son? Is this the one you say was born blind? How is it he can now see?"

"We know he is our son," the parents answered, "and we know he was born blind. But how he can see now, or who opened his eyes, we don't know. Ask him. He is of age; he will speak for himself."

At the first word, he had recognized them. A lifetime of blindness had made him attentive to voices and these were unmistakably the ones of his parents. His newly-healed eyes welled with tears as he took in their appearance. The man was tall and slender with angular features and wavy hair. She was short and fair-skinned. He looked at his arms and decided that he must favor his mother, a statement he remembered hearing from his youth.

He loved them dearly, and he had only recently moved away from them to try living alone. Now they were in a precarious position. All of their lives, they had lived with the burden of rumors that their sins had been the reason for their son's blindness. Now the Pharisees were trying to entrap them. They wished to see if his parents were followers of Jesus who maybe took their son to Him for healing. If so, they would be expelled from the synagogue.

Although the blind man had not known it, the previous day Jesus had nearly been stoned near the temple for saying that He had lived before Abraham, and the priests had issued an order that no one would be allowed to sacrifice if they acknowledged Jesus as Christ. Now he and his parents were caught in a struggle between Jesus and the religious leaders.

Tired of questioning his parents, the Pharisees turned their attention back to the healed man. He wanted only to be left alone so that he could embrace his parents, now shaking and crying in the rear of the temple, but he knew that he must show respect to their questions to keep them from harming his parents any more.

"Give glory to God. We know this man is a sinner," the Pharisees told him. They were wanting his story to omit Jesus entirely so they would not be faced with the awkward question of where Jesus got His power.

Patiently, he answered them. "Whether He is a sinner or not, I don't know. One thing I do know. I was blind but now I see!"

"What did He do to you? How did He open your eyes?" Their questions were becoming repetitious, and he was starting to tire of them.

He answered, "I have told you already and you did not listen. Why do you want to hear it again? Do you want to become His disciples too?" That last remark had not been a particularly wise one to make, but in his anger he couldn't resist trying to make them see how foolish they looked in their attempts to deny the obvious.

"You are this fellow's disciple! We are disciples of Moses! We know that God spoke to Moses, but as for this fellow, we don't even know where He comes from," they said.

Several hours ago, the healed man had been angry at the Rabbi called Jesus for putting mud in his eyes. Now he found himself defending Him.

"Now that is remarkable! You don't know where He comes from, yet He opened my eyes. If this man were not from God He could do nothing."

The Pharisees, having no reply to his logic, retreated to familiar ground. "You were steeped in sin at birth! How dare you lecture us!" With that, they threw him out of the temple, banning him forever from worshiping there.

Jesus, meanwhile, had heard about the commotion caused by His morning miracle and arrived at the temple just as the healed man was being evicted.

Walking up to him, Jesus asked, "Do you believe in the Son of Man?"

The healed man straightened his robe from the jostling he had received as he looked up at Jesus. He was desperately looking for something to believe in. He wanted no part of the religion of those who had just thrown him out of the temple.

"Who is He, sir? Tell me so that I may believe in Him."

Jesus said, "You have now seen Him; in fact, He is the

One speaking with you."

Realizing for the first time that this was Jesus, the healed man fell to his knees and worshiped Him, saying, "Lord, I believe."

As he knelt at the feet of Jesus, he heard Him teach a short lesson on spiritual blindness to the Pharisees. Remembering the statement from that morning about Jesus being light, he realized for the first time what He had meant. One is only blind if one cannot see the Light.

CHAPTER FOURTEEN

"LORD IF YOU HAD BEEN HERE . . . ."

Ever felt abandoned by God? If so, you're in good company. Jesus felt that way on the cross when He cried out, "My God, My God! Why have You forsaken Me?"

"Where are You, God?" It's not an impertinent question to ask. Sometimes He feels far away. When death takes away a loved one, or sickness invades a healthy body, it's a natural question to ask. If God had only been close enough to hear my prayers, none of this would have happened, we think.

Mary, the sister of Lazarus, finds herself with these same nagging doubts when Jesus arrives four days after Lazarus has died. She confronts Him in the story below, verbalizing the feelings that countless others have had since: "Where were You when I needed You?"

The sisters had called for Jesus six days ago. At that time, their brother, Lazarus, was on his deathbed with a fever the doctors could not cure. Only thirty years old, Lazarus was now gone—the fever had taken him four days ago. And still, there was no sign of Jesus.

Lazarus had lived with Mary and Martha, his unmarried sisters, and provided for them. In return, they kept his house, prepared his meals and made his clothing. The three had been friends of Jesus, following Him when He was in the region, and hosting Him in their home for a meal.

The younger of the two, Mary, had a special relationship with the Master. On one occasion, when He had visited her home, Mary wanted only to sit at His feet and listen to His teachings, while Martha busily prepared the meal. Jesus had rescued her from criticism by telling Martha that Mary had made the right choice in listening to Him rather than being distracted by the preparations.

But Mary was now confused. Nearly a week ago, she had requested that Jesus hurry to their home in Bethany to heal Lazarus. She had seen Him perform numerous healings in the past, and she was certain that He would hurry to Lazarus' bed when He got the simple message, "Lord, the one You love is sick."

When He got the message, Jesus was not in the region of Judea. He had left Jerusalem after the Jews there had threatened to stone Him for blasphemy. As they attempted to seize Him and His apostles, He had crossed the Jordan to safety. It had been their closest brush with the anger of the Pharisees so far. Now Jesus received word from Mary's messenger that He must go back to where the Jews were attempting to kill Him. Yet

He knew that His time on Earth was not yet up.

As Jesus contemplated the trip, He allowed two more days to pass. He weighed the grief that Mary and Martha must be bearing against the fear that His apostles would feel when He told them of His plans. Finally, He revealed His plan to the apostles, saying, "Our friend Lazarus has fallen asleep, but I am going to wake him up." Not understanding the message, and not wanting to go back into Judea, the apostles asked why Lazarus could not awake on his own. Jesus explained, "Lazarus is dead, and for your sake I am glad I was not there, so that you may believe. But let us go to him."

The apostles were frightened and shocked at His announcement. Hadn't they just escaped with their lives two days earlier? Many of them fully expected to never go back to Judea, and certainly not within days after they were nearly killed. As they pondered whether to go back to Bethany, Thomas voiced the sentiment on their minds, "Let us also go, that we may die with Him." So the Twelve, expecting the worst, turned towards Judea, the recent escape fresh on their minds.

Meanwhile, Mary's hope had turned to despair. The Lord had failed to come. Her brother had died and had been buried now for four days. She wept at her loss, and she wept from a sense of betrayal. Why hadn't He come? He had healed total strangers. Why hadn't He come to heal one that He loved? Where was He now in their most desperate hour? She wanted answers to these questions, but could find none.

As they approached Bethany, the apostles began to feel a sense of relief. They had crossed the Jordan two days ago, and had not experienced any troubles yet. Although Bethany was only a short walk from the potential trouble in Jerusalem, it was also the home of some of the Lord's most fervent followers. Surely nothing would happen to them in Bethany.

The first resident who ran to greet them informed Jesus that Lazarus had been dead for four days, something the Lord had told the Twelve before they crossed the Jordan. They marveled at how He knew, though little about the Master surprised them anymore.

The crowds gathering at their house informed the sisters that Jesus would soon be inside the city. Martha prepared to go and meet Him, but Mary chose to stay behind. What could she possibly say to Him? She had so much she wanted to say, yet it was not her place to criticize the Lord. Deep in her heart, she knew that He could have prevented the death if He had come. Why did He choose not to? Yet, did she dare ask Him such an impertinent question?

Martha, in her usual manner, went first and greeted the Lord before He entered the city. Her confrontation with Him was quick and direct. Jesus handled her questions with love and assurances, then asked for Mary. Martha went back to her home to get her younger sister.

When the sisters returned together, Jesus had still not entered the city. The apostles waited uneasily beside the road. They would have preferred being in the houses of Bethany to this open road less than two miles from the spot where they were nearly stoned in Jerusalem. Whatever Jesus was going to do, they wished that He would hurry up and do it, and take shelter with some of His followers in their homes. But they knew from experience that Jesus could not be rushed when He was dealing with people.

Mary had left her home hurriedly. As was the custom, the mourners followed her, thinking that she was going to the tomb. As Mary walked to where the Master waited, she rehearsed what she would say, changing the words with every attempt. What could she say? The question gnawed at her.

When she came to Jesus, she fell at His feet and wept. The only words that came out were not the ones she rehearsed. Instead, they were the ones directly from her heart, "Lord, if You had been here, my brother would not have died."

The words were the same ones Martha had said earlier. Yet when Mary blurted them out, crying at the Master's feet, they moved Jesus to tears. As He cried, the apostles huddled among themselves. They asked each other if any had ever seen an open display of emotion like this from Jesus. They had seen Him angry when He drove the vendors from the temple. And they had heard Him raise His voice to the Pharisees on more than one occasion, including the time a few days ago that had nearly got Him and all of them stoned to death. Yet this was a side of Jesus they hadn't seen.

The apostles wondered what it meant. A few secretly pondered if His ability to establish a kingdom would be hindered if He allowed His emotions to overrule His logic. They shouldn't even be out in the open right now, yet here they were, surrounded by the Jewish friends who had followed Mary, and Jesus was crying.

While the apostles conferred, Mary continued to weep at the feet of Jesus. After a while, Jesus asked to see the tomb, and was led there. When He got to the tomb, He ordered the stone to be rolled away. Thinking that Jesus wished to view the body, Martha reminded Him that he had been dead four days. She knew that the modest amount of spices and wrappings that they had been able to afford would only last a day or two at most in the heat.

Overruling her protest, Jesus again ordered the stone to be removed, looked up to heaven and prayed, and called out in a loud voice, "Lazarus, come out!" To the amazement of the crowd, Lazarus came out. Still clothed in burial linen, Lazarus blinked at the bright sunlight and tugged at the strips of cloth that dangled from his arms and feet, and dragged behind him as he walked.

The last person to look was Mary, who still had her face buried on Jesus' shoulder, leaning on Him for support. She was afraid to look, yet wanted to. By the time that she looked, she got a glimpse of his back as some of the men from Bethany were leading him away to find him food and suitable clothing. She buried her face on His shoulder again as she wept in joy and relief at the sight of her brother.

The crowd followed Lazarus. Martha thanked Jesus and muttered an apology for her lack of faith, then turned in the direction of her home. Lazarus must be fed, and there would be an inevitable stream of visitors, meaning that she had many preparations to make, and she knew from experience that she couldn't count on

Mary for any help.

The Twelve followed the crowd as well, preferring the safety of numbers to staying on the outskirts of town. They knew this miracle would keep them safe in Bethany for a while, since no one would risk crowd reaction by attempting to take Jesus now.

Soon Mary and Jesus were all alone. There, outside of Bethany, she poured her heart out to Him. Where had He been in the hour of her greatest need? Why did she not get her help from Him on her own schedule and not His?

He talked to her of life and death, resurrection and eternity. He told her that His miracles were not only to ease the current human condition, but also to glorify God and make others believe. The resurrection of Lazarus had all been a part of that plan, He said, in a way that simply healing him could have never accomplished. Her unanswered petition had not been a rejection; it simply had not fit into the eternal plan.

She was not the first to wonder where God was during a time of crisis, He said, and she would not be the last. It was not wrong to ask the questions, He said. There is a difference between questioning and doubt. Mary had never doubted. She had simply questioned. However, He added, some questions would never be answered in this life. Faith, He said, was the only temporary relief for the burning questions of eternity.

With that, they stood and walked to the house where Martha was tending to Lazarus, and where the apostles were discussing how to convince the Master to leave under cover of dark.

The woman pours her
perfume at the feet of Jesus.

CHAPTER FIFTEEN

A GOAT BECOMES A LAMB

Who knows how the downtrodden of the world get there? The homeless once took crayons and drew dream houses on paper. The alcoholic was once a young man dressing for his first date; the unwed mother once a young girl combing the hair of a doll. Few are born in the gutter, yet many find their way there. Jesus had a knack for finding people wherever life had taken them and lifting them up. In fact, he once said that the well had no need for a physician and that he intended to seek out the spiritually sick.

No more moving story exists in the Scriptures than the story of the woman of ill-repute wiping the Master's feet with her hair and her tears. It's loved because each of us has played most of the roles in the story at some time in our lives.

We've been the sinner, unable to look Jesus in the eye and wishing only to beg for mercy at His feet. We've been the self righteous who look at the homeless, the drug-addicted or the poor in the same manner the dinner guests looked upon the woman. We've been Simon, who wanted to bask in the re-flected glory of Jesus by having Him in his home. Each time we make sure that others see our good deeds and give us cred-it.

What follows is how one woman may have slid into the depths of despair and how Christ pulled her out.

She awoke well after the middle of the day, alone in her bed. She worked at night and awakened to regret each morning. This was not the life she wanted to lead—the life of a prostitute—but it was the only one she was now forced to lead.

She had been engaged once, but her love changed his mind about the upcoming marriage. Her father, though keeping up good appearances in the community of Bethany, was actually deep in debt and unable to provide any dowry of substance for his daughter's wedding. Her fiance lost interest as soon as he found out that she would come into the marriage penniless.

Since Jewish engagements were virtually as binding as marriage vows, her husband-to-be lied to break his commitment. To save face in the community, he claimed that he was ending the period of engagement because she was not a virgin. It was a malicious and false claim, but one believed by most. Her father took advantage of the opportunity to disown, her giving him one less mouth to feed, and no other man would have her.

Her father died soon afterwards. Her mother moved away and never contacted her again. She turned to the streets for employment. Her would-be husband quickly married another, though she got secret pleasure in knowing that he frequented her friends who were also prostitutes. He was one of the few people she knew who had sunk lower than she had, and she felt that she had somehow reached the bottom with more honor than he.

But that had been several years ago, and now she wanted out of the abyss. She looked much older today than when she became a prostitute. One aged fast in her profession. Already she was finding it harder to keep up the lifestyle, and lately she had even had trouble interesting men with her looks. That fact had been gnawing at her now for months. She was a decent person in an indecent person's profession. She was aging while men looked for youth. Somehow there must be a way out of this mess of a life she was living.

So on this morning when she lay on the bed, fighting off the bright rays of the sun penetrating through the cracks in the window covers, she was contemplating her life. And for the first time, she was also contemplating ending it. She had a bad past and no promise of a better future. Time wasn't kind to aging prostitutes, she knew that from watching the others.

As she sat thinking about these things, she heard the commotion outside. The voices said that the one called Jesus was coming to Bethany that very day. She remembered the name. He had come to Bethany before, drawing large crowds to hear His teaching. Some said that He even healed the sick and caused blind men to see. Perhaps He might hold the answer, she thought.

Scrambling to her feet to dress, she spotted for the first time the gift left for her by her client from the previous night, an alabaster jar of perfume. The imported fragrance was expensive–probably more than a year's wages for an ordinary laborer. The small vial came on a leather string so that it could be worn around the neck, as many of the wealthier ladies did. She also knew what the gift meant. He would never return. After visiting her weekly for years, his graceful exit was this extravagant gift. She had seen it before and she recognized it now. He had been almost her sole source of income for the past two years, and now he wouldn't be back. She knew that he had left it behind to give her something of value to support her until she found someone else.

But as she slipped the perfume around her neck, she felt beautiful again. She had seen the wealthier ladies in town wear these vials before, but never thought she would own one. She probably would have to sell it tomorrow. Today she would enjoy it.

Walking outside, she blinked at the sun's rays, surprised that it was well after midday. She hadn't eaten, but she wasn't hungry. She was anxious to follow the last ones making their way to the small hill outside of town where she would get a glimpse of the One she had heard about before.

When she reached the crowd, she stopped at the edge. Years of experience had taught her that women of her profession didn't belong at the front of any crowd. She didn't dare risk confrontation with the Pharisees or any other of the leaders of Bethany. She left them alone and they left her alone. Trying to get one of the best locations to hear Jesus was an invitation to a confrontation that she didn't want. Prostitutes belonged in the back of the crowd along with the old and feeble.

She fingered the vial of perfume as she strained to hear the voice of Jesus. As He taught, the crowd became quiet. He was speaking in stories, easy to understand. She listened as He told a story of ten virgins waiting for the bridegroom. She remembered her own bad experience at marriage. He told another story about a man that gave his servants talents to invest in his absence. It reminded her that she must wisely invest the money from the gift she now wore around her neck. It would have to last her a long time.

His final story was about sheep and goats. As she listened, Jesus applied the story by saying that a time would come when God would do the same thing with His people that a shepherd did with his flocks. Only the separation that God would make would be based on kindness, hospitality and generosity. On the one hand would be the sheep, who had all these qualities, and on the other hand would be the goats, who had none of them.

As she looked around the crowd with the wisdom of the street, she saw all types. There were the true sheep, the righteous who tried to live upright. She had little contact with them. There were the true goats who lived only for evil. She had met plenty of those in her day.

But there was yet another category that she despised even more—the false sheep who were really goats. She knew these people well. They acted like sheep in the day, but they came to her at night. They would make their profits by foreclosing on widows, and then proudly tithe in the temple for all to see.

None of these categories fit her, however. She was a

different type. To others, she was a goat, and she knew they were right. Her lifestyle was undeniable. But inside, she felt like a sheep. Only she knew her heart. Only she knew of her private acts of generosity to the fringe people of society that congregated in her area of town. She didn't have the social status of the Pharisees, but neither was she guilty of their hypocrisy. She would always be a goat to them, but she longed to be as pure and white as one of the sheep.

She continued to watch as some in the crowd came forward to be healed. She noticed that as He healed them, He also forgave their sins. The Pharisees began to argue with Him over this point, but it was hard to deny that One who had the power to heal diseases could also forgive sins. Recognizing that they were in the minority and out of favor with the crowds, the Pharisees retreated to plot a way to stop Him.

As the crowds began to disperse, she heard some expressing surprise that Jesus had accepted an invitation to eat at the home of Simon of the Pharisees that evening. She knew the home—it was one of the most fashionable in a part of the city where people like her seldom went. What could she do to make herself fit to speak to Jesus?

She ran to Simon's house and waited for hours in the shadow of the porch at the rear. When she heard the party enter, she listened as Simon loudly greeted each of his guests. It was obvious that Simon was enjoying the attention focused on him as the host of the One whose works and teachings were on everyone's lips. To her, Simon was a goat, and she resented the fact that she had to hide in the gathering shadows to meet Jesus while a hypocrite like Simon didn't.

Finally, she heard Simon welcome Jesus to his house. The entire group was then seated at the table in Simon's courtyard. He was hosting the meal in the open for all the community to see his good fortune at having a personal visit by Jesus. He didn't believe His claim that He was the Son of God, but Simon liked the attention that Jesus' notoriety brought.

Before the servants could bring the meal, the woman slipped out of the shadows of the alley to speak to Jesus. Quickly stepping inside the gate, she walked directly to Him. Standing beside Him, she realized that words were not going to come. Huge tears welled in her eyes as her lifetime of sin weighed heavy on her. Her tears fell on His feet, which were still dusty from the walk. Embarrassed, she stooped to wipe her tears off.

As she knelt, her perfume dangled from the leather string. She reached for the bottle. It was all the security she had in life, but that meant little for a life as worthless as hers. With one hand, she poured the perfume on His feet. With the other, she let down her long brown hair.

Some in the party gasped at the extravagance of the perfume, others at the brazenness of a woman letting down her hair in public. She didn't hear them, nor would she have cared. Using the mixture of tears and perfume, she began to wipe his feet clean with her hair.

Simon had watched her entrance in disbelief and had summoned a servant to remove her. By the time He came, however, it was evident that Jesus was allowing her to proceed, so Simon waved the servant off. This just confirmed to Simon what he already thought about Jesus. He might be some sort of healer, but He had no special prophetic powers. He couldn't even recognize a common prostitute when He saw one. His thoughts were interrupted by Jesus.

"Simon, I have something to tell you."

"Tell me, Teacher," he said.

As she continued to wipe His feet, Jesus amazed Simon by challenging his private thoughts. He told a story about forgiveness and then turned His attention to the woman at His feet.

"Do you see this woman? I came into your house. You did not give Me any water for My feet, but she wet My feet with her tears and wiped them with her hair. You did not give Me a kiss, but this woman, from the time I entered, has not stopped kissing My feet. You did not pour oil on My head, but she has poured perfume on My feet. Therefore I tell you, her many sins have been forgiven—for she loved much. But he who has been forgiven little loves little."

Turning her face to His, Jesus looked at her and said, "Your sins are forgiven."

For the first time in years, she felt clean. Clean as a pure, white lamb. She wanted to stay at His feet, but she could already hear the muttering of others at the table about the audacity of Jesus to presume to forgive her sins. She didn't doubt it, however. This feeling was too real to be a fraud. She realized, though, that it was time to go. Her lifestyle had trained her to feel hot stares behind her back, and she felt that now.

But as she stood to leave, Jesus spoke to her one more time.

"Your faith has saved you; go in peace."

She would not see Him again. Weeks later, she heard that He had been crucified in Jerusalem, but that some said He was not dead. She smiled when she heard it. He was alive, she thought. He was alive in every goat who aspired to be a lamb.

CHAPTER SIXTEEN

CLEAN FROM THE INSIDE OUT

How would you like to have to announce your biggest flaw or your darkest secret to total strangers? Perhaps wear a pin that says "Child of a broken home" on your lapel? Or have a business card that says "Filed for bankruptcy."

That was the situation facing lepers during Jesus' day. Just in case someone didn't get the message from their outer appearance, Jewish law demanded that the lepers call out "Unclean!" to any passersby to avoid spreading their loathsome disease throughout the population.

Naturally, the general population was not required to call out their inadequacies in return. No one was forced to yell, "cheater" or "adulterer" or "gossip" when they approached the leper colony.

Scripture tells us that we were all once "unclean," and have only been cleansed by the blood of Christ. But all too often, we forget to thank God for how good it feels to be clean because we've forgotten how bad it felt to be unclean. It's easy to forget. Only one of the ten lepers in this story returned to thank Jesus.

Paul never forgot his unclean past. He didn't dwell on it, but he didn't forget it either, because it reminded him of just how good it felt to be clean.

The leper often thought how ironic it was that he, a Samaritan, was associating with Jewish lepers who would have nothing to do with him if only they were clean. He joked with them that he'd be a leper to them even if all of them were healthy, so it was fortunate for him that they weren't. They laughed in agreement, but deep inside, they knew it was true. Leprosy was the great equalizer that had brought them all together.

Today, however, the Samaritan didn't know what to make of his Jewish friends. As he watched, one of them ran to the others and told them of a group of travelers approaching. Normally, this was nothing to get excited about. In fact it was a nuisance to have to cover one's face and yell out "Unclean!" But lately, even the Samaritan had taken to doing it, mostly just to be like the others.

But as this group approached, the Jews acted as if they knew the traveler. Furthermore, they acted as if they were glad He was approaching. Then, when they began to shout, they called Him by name. "Jesus," they said. Others called Him "Jesus, Master." This surprised the Samaritan, who had known these Jews long enough to know that when you're a leper, you hold very little to be sacred. If life spits on you, you spit right back on it. These men had never called anyone Master before, not even the occasional priest who ventured into the camp to perform religious ceremonies for the other nine.

Not only were they calling Him by name, and acknowledging Him as Master, they were asking Him to have pity on them. What could this mean? Surely everyone had pity on them, he thought. What's not to pity? He was serving a life sentence in a leper colony with no hope of getting out. However, by the urgency of their calling, he figured that they must mean monetary pity. They were begging for money to spend on wine, he thought. Quickly he joined in, not even knowing Whom he was addressing. "Jesus, Master, have pity on us."

This Jesus approached close enough to talk to them, far closer than any of the others ever did, the Samaritan thought. He is going to be good for enough money for everyone to get drunk, he thought.

"Go show yourselves to the priests," Jesus said to the ten, and immediately the other nine began to run in the direction of the village.

The Samaritan, however, stood stunned. A moment earlier he was anticipating an evening with enough wine to make him forget his troubles for awhile, and now he watched in disbelief as his fellow lepers ran toward the village, where they could be executed for entering the city gates. He started to ask a few questions, but decided to run first and get his answers later. Maybe the stranger named Jesus had thrown some money on the ground and he had missed it. They might be going to buy wine without him right now. He took off running after the others, eager to catch them.

Soon, the Samaritan caught the nine, who had slowed

to the pace of the oldest in the group. As they continued to run, the Samaritan noticed a miracle occurring before his eyes. They were being cleansed of their leprosy! The others acted less surprised than he, yet no less joyful.

"You knew!" he shouted. "How did you know! Who told you He was a healer?" the Samaritan asked. He had heard their stories at night of the powers of their prophets like Elijah and Elisha, but he had never expected to encounter one.

"He's Jesus of Nazareth," one said. "He's turned water to wine and raised the dead," said another. "He goes all over. Heals the sick. Feeds people too," said another. "Claims to get His power from God," another said.

"I don't care where He got His power. I'm just glad He used a little on us," the Samaritan shouted to a rousing round of cheers.

Within minutes, they all tired of running and the city was still far down the road. "Let's split up and go our own ways now," said one, looking back to make sure that Jesus was nowhere in sight. "That would be the wise thing to do," said another.

"Wait," said the Samaritan. "Aren't you supposed to go into the village and show yourself to the priest?" He didn't include himself in this question since he knew he would never be allowed in the temple.

"Can't do it. Too risky," explained the oldest of his Jewish friends. "The law only has instructions for how to treat a leper once he's sick. They don't ever figure you're going to get well. If we go back, they'll accuse us of sorcery or worse. We're no good to them clean. Too much to explain."

"But if we go up the road a bit, change towns, get a new identity, no one will be the wiser," said another.

"But couldn't you just tell the priest about Jesus?" asked the Samaritan.

"They know about Him," said a Jew who had only been in the camp for a couple of months, "and they don't believe in Him. We'd really be in trouble if we mentioned that He healed us. We can't win either way."

"So Jesus won't get the credit for what He did today?"

"Afraid not."

"Shouldn't we go back and thank Him, at least?"

"Well, you can, but I'm not going to take a chance. Besides, He might ask if we went to the priest. I don't want to get a man like that mad at me."

The others agreed and, in groups of twos and threes, went in different directions where they could stay with relatives and discreetly start a new life. Each bid the others goodbye, and each made a special note of telling the Samaritan farewell.

Soon, the Samaritan was left alone. Though his skin was clean, he still felt dirty. Why had he been chosen? Was he deserving of such a gift? Had the healer known He was cleansing a Samaritan? Did he dare accept such a gift without thanking the One they called Master?

He sat down to think. The trip to the priest was definitely out. No Samaritan could go into the temple, and surely none could get an audience with the priest. Strange, he thought, in their eyes, I'm still dirty even though I'm clean. Yet something still gnawed at the

Samaritan. He had never felt so torn—clean, yet dirty, fortunate, yet undeserving.

Then it came to him. He'd present himself to the only One he was sure would accept him—the Master who had cleansed him. He quickly turned and ran back in the direction of Jesus' party. When he reached them, he knelt down and praised God, remembering that one of them had said that the Master's powers came from the One they called Jehovah. Then he heard the Master speak.

"Were not all ten cleansed? Where are the other nine? Was no one found to return and give praise except this foreigner?"

Then, turning and looking directly into the eyes of the Samaritan, He said, "Rise and go, your faith has made you well."

As he rose, he felt the same sensation he had felt earlier. Cleansed again, inside and out! And as he watched Jesus and His apostles walk away into the distance, something inside told him that he would never feel dirty or unworthy again.

CHAPTER SEVENTEEN

"ONE THING YOU LACK. . . ."

The last time I got a speeding ticket, I was righteously indignant. I had observed the law (with a small fudge factor) all afternoon and only had sped up within ten minutes of getting the ticket because I had a carsick puppy in the back seat and we needed a town and paper towels badly.

Smarting from the ticket, I called the judge later and pleaded my case to no avail. What I wanted was credit for all the miles I had driven within the law. What I got was judgment for the few miles I drove outside the limits of the law.

The young man in the story below had a similar problem. He wanted credit for the laws he had already kept. Jesus demanded far more.

When you look at this story, you can see the attraction of the law, and why Paul had to fight the Judaizing Christians in virtually every one of his epistles. The law limits my liability: do this much and no more. The demands of self-sacrifice, however, never end.

And every time I try to tell God that I've taught my Bible class, given my contribution and done my witnessing, He comes back gently and says, "This one thing you lack."

The young man had lacked for nothing his entire life. The only son of a wealthy Jewish merchant, he had sat clothed in imported linen at the feet of the finest teachers of the Law. Servants had tended to him since birth. Even now, as a young man, he had never performed some of the mundane tasks of life such as saddling a donkey or gathering fuel wood. There was not one thing he wanted that he lacked in life.

His life was the embodiment of current Jewish theology: God had been good to him because he had been good to God. Like his father before him, he had studied the Law since early childhood, and had meticulously kept all its commandments. And the wealth that he enjoyed was evidence in the community of the good life that he lived.

The young man had heard about the Teacher Who was telling the crowds about the possibility of eternal life. He was intrigued. In his mind, eternal life would be simply a continuation of the favored status he currently enjoyed in life, a scenario that excited him. When he heard that Jesus had crossed the Jordan and would be coming through his region, he decided to meet the Teacher to ask Him about this eternal life.

As he set out at dawn for the shore, he wondered what the price would be for the secret to eternal life. Surely he could pay it. And it would be a good investment, since death was the only cloud on his otherwise unblemished future. He pondered that thought for a moment: an unending life lacking for nothing.

By mid-morning when he found the Teacher, the crowds had already grown large. As the young man arrived, Jesus was teaching on divorce, prompted by a question posed to Him by the Pharisees. He then spoke to the crowd in parables, telling a story about a persistent widow who petitioned a judge repeatedly for vindication. The young man could relate to that. Among his father's holdings were the houses of several widows who never seemed to have anything to do except complain to their landlord.

The Teacher told another story about a Pharisee and a tax collector. The young man thought it odd that the tax collector was the righteous one in the story. He and his father had nothing but trouble with tax collectors.

As the young man watched, several parents brought small children to the Teacher to be blessed. The ones called His apostles attempted to stop the parents, urging them to take the children away. When He saw what was happening, Jesus openly rebuked His apostles saying, "Let the little children come to Me and do not hinder them, for the kingdom of God belongs to such as these. I tell you the truth, anyone who will not receive the kingdom of God like a little child will never enter it." Having said that, Jesus turned His attention to the children, touching them and saying a blessing over each.

The stories and the display of compassion by the Teacher moved the young man to ask his question about eternal life. Taking the words of Jesus to heart, the young man stepped forward and fell on his knees before Jesus, just as a child. "Good Teacher," he asked, "What must I do to inherit eternal life?"

Looking down at the young man, Jesus saw that he was different from the lame and blind and poor that followed Him daily. This young man had no need of food, and he was in good health. The crowd had parted to let him through, obviously recognizing his stature in the region on this side of the Jordan.

"Why do you call Me good?" Jesus answered. "No one is good—except God alone." The young man, still kneeling, silently nodded his head in acknowledgement that he had intentionally called Him "good" and that he knew he was in the presence of God. Suddenly, this trip that had begun as a casual quest to obtain what he could not buy with his wealth had turned serious. He felt the eyes of hundreds in the crowd on him as He now waited for the answer to His question. By bowing as a child, and acknowledging Jesus as Lord, he had put himself in a position he had never been in, and he felt awkward and vulnerable.

The blind and the lame, they had nothing to lose by prostrating themselves before the Teacher. But he could lose his status in the community if he were made to look foolish. Moments earlier, the Teacher had been indignant with His own apostles. What if he became indignant now? The young man's heart pounded in his chest as Jesus let the first words linger. What if Jesus rebuked him in front of all these people?

Jesus continued. "You know the commandments: 'Do not murder, do not commit adultery, do not steal, do not give false testimony, do not defraud, honor your father and mother.' "

The young man breathed a sigh of relief. He had done all these things as a normal part of growing up in an orthodox Jewish home. If this was all there was to obtaining eternal life, he was sure to be rewarded.

"Teacher," he declared, "all these I have kept since I was a boy."

As he kneeled at the Teacher's feet, he looked up, expecting praise for his orthodoxy. Giving him a look of love, Jesus continued. "One thing you lack," He said. His hopes rose. Only one more law to keep, and eternal life was his!

"Go, sell everything you have and give it to the poor, and you will have treasure in heaven. Then come, follow Me."

The words stung his heart like the redness stung his face. The young man had never lacked for anything in his life. If he did, he bought it immediately. Yet now he lacked something. He lacked what it took to inherit eternal life. And to get it would cost him everything that he had.

That was too high a price to pay. And, worse still, he must now get up and walk through the crowds again, this time more humbly than before. As he rose to walk away, he heard the Teacher say to His listeners: "How hard it is for the rich to enter the kingdom of God!"

There was that phrase again: the kingdom of God. Hadn't the Teacher said that it was possible for a child to enter in? Sure, he thought, children have nothing to lose. Neither do the lame, the blind or the poor. If they want to act childish, who cares? But he had wealth and status and grown-up responsibilities. He couldn't act like a child and throw all that away.

As the rich young man walked away, through crowds that scarcely moved to let him through, he heard the Teacher call the children back to Him again. Jesus continued teaching them, using him as an illustration.

"Children, how hard it is to enter the kingdom of God! It is easier for a camel to go through the eye of a needle than for a rich man to enter the kingdom of God."

The children giggled at the outrageousness of the analogy, imagining in their minds a Jewish tailor attempting to get an entire camel through his sewing needle. Wouldn't it get stuck between the humps, one asked, sending the others into another round of laughter. But Jesus wasn't smiling. On His face was an expression of love and pity as He watched the young man leave to return to the earthly wealth that he loved more than heavenly riches.

CHAPTER EIGHTEEN

A Life Made Full by an Empty Tomb

Where I formerly taught, I knew a young man whose father was slowly dying from a degenerative disease. At the same time, the student and his fiance were planning their wedding. Finally the day arrived, but his father's health was failing. In fact, he died quietly, unobserved by most of the guests, during the ceremony.

Imagine the lowest low and the highest high of your life occurring within minutes of each other and you'll know how he felt.

A similar experience happened to the four women who made their way to the tomb of Jesus in the early dawn, only to find it empty.

The martyr was a Savior! The sad story was now the Good News! What an emotional roller coaster that must have been.

In some ways, I think we've been deprived by hearing of the death and resurrection of Jesus as historical fact in a single story. To have lived it over that long Sabbath day and night

*and to experience the agony and exhilaration almost simulta-
neously would be, I think, a life-changing experience for us
all. It certainly was for these four women and for the eleven
apostles. What follows is what feeling might have passed
through the mind of the one witness about whom we know the
least.*

Though it would not be dawn for another hour, Joanna moved quickly about her house, aided by the dim,
flickering light from a single oil lamp. The cottage was
comfortable for a widow such as Joanna. She was left
well-off by her late husband.

A close friend of Mary of Magdala, Joanna had been
drawn to Jesus by association with her friend. With
Mary, Joanna had watched while He healed the sick,
cast out demons and raised the dead. She had heard the
teachings and had been baptized by John. Tears came to
her eyes as she gathered the spices and perfumes she
had stored away since her husband's burial. This morning would close another chapter in her life, as she
would go with Mary Magdalene, Mary the mother of
James, and Salome to give Jesus a proper Jewish burial.

Joanna had watched at the foot of the cross as Jesus
had been crucified by the Roman soldiers. She had only
been steps away from His mother when Jesus looked
down on her from the cross and called for His apostle
John to care for her as a son would.

She had seen the sky turn dark and she had watched
as the soldiers drove the spear in His side to assure that
He was dead. In the end, only the women and John had
remained at the cross until the very end. The other
apostles had fled to safety. Most of the followers had

lost heart and left. Even those who came to jeer lost interest when they felt Jesus no longer heard their taunts. But Joanna and the other women had stayed, following the burial detachment to the tomb which had been supplied by Joseph of Arimathea, a member of the Council who had not consented to the killing of Jesus.

She had examined the tomb, and had watched as Joseph wrapped the body in a clean linen cloth, which quickly became red with blood. A separate cloth was placed over His face. This was not a ceremonial burial, but it would have to do until after the Sabbath. There had been nothing else they could do. The Sabbath would start at sundown, and the spices and clothing they needed were in the city below. They had watched as Joseph and another man strained to roll the stone into place before the opening of the tomb.

At that point, Joanna and the others made their way down in the deepening darkness. The footpath leading to Jerusalem was barely visible. The muffled cries of Jesus' mother could be heard as she held tightly to John. Before they reached the bottom, he would be carrying her. He would take her home and spend the Sabbath there with her. Mary of Magdala was invited to the house of Salome. Though they invited Joanna, she refused. This was one Sabbath when she preferred to be alone with her thoughts.

During the long day that followed, Joanna's mind was seldom on the Sabbath. As the hours passed, she reflected on the three years of frequent trips she made to stand among the crowds as Jesus taught. Her occasional personal meetings with the Master in the home of Mary, mother of James, were foremost among those treasured memories. She had been happier in those last three years than in any of the twelve years since her husband had died. She had been inspired by His teachings and amazed by His miracles. Surely, she thought, He had been one of God's most powerful prophets. But now it was over, and soon she would go anoint His body and close the tomb for the final time.

While He was on the earth, many schools of thought arose about who Jesus was. Some said He was a prophet. Others thought that perhaps He was the reincarnation of Elijah, who many thought would return to life again. To others He was a master teacher, a Rabbi without peer. Mary Magdalene frequently called Him "Rabboni," the Aramaic name for Teacher. Many had hoped that He would be the Deliverer who would lead them out from under Roman rule. A few even felt that He was the Messiah, the Son of God Who had been prophesied in the Scriptures.

Though some of her friends thought that Jesus was the Messiah, Joanna had always been convinced that He was a prophet empowered with special gifts from God. As deeply as she loved her friends, and as much as she wanted to believe that Jesus was the Son of God in the flesh, Joanna could not fully accept a God who would allow Himself to be treated unjustly by men.

She had seen Him nearly stoned and forced to flee across the Jordan. She had witnessed the crucifixion. Surely God would not have allowed the hated Romans to spit on Him and slap Him. The God of Moses would have ordered fire from heaven or caused the earth to swallow such men up. Jesus was special, she thought, but He was not God. In Joanna's mind, God could not be killed by men.

Finally, it was light. By working in the dark, Joanna was ready to leave as soon as there was enough light to follow the rocky path leading to the burial area. Joanna left her house and walked the street to Salome's house, where the others were waiting. Like Joanna, they had been up for hours and were now anxious to leave with their load of linen, perfume and spices supplied by Nicodemus to complete the ceremonial burial cut short by the advent of the Sabbath.

The women had heard that the tomb would be sealed and guarded. The Romans had taken this precaution on the Sabbath after the chief priests of the Jews had consulted with Pilate. They had asked for the guard lest someone come and steal the body and claim that He had been raised from the dead. Pilate had consented gladly. He would have enough problems with those who would make Jesus into a martyr without dealing with those who would make Him into a god.

The women discussed this new dilemma as they walked. They hoped that they could convince the guards to roll the stone away for them. Surely four Jewish women would not be perceived as a threat to the Roman guards. They would do their work quickly and return to Jerusalem by mid-morning.

Without cooperation from the guards, the task was going to be impossible. Each of the women knew that, but none of them discussed it. Even if they were given permission to enter the tomb, the stone was too heavy for the three of them to roll, and it had been rolled into a rut in front of the tomb, meaning that it would have to be lifted with a long stick acting as a lever as it was rolled. Their only hope was to touch the soldiers with their request, and then hope that the men were sufficient for the task.

The tomb donated by Joseph was hewn straight into the mountain. The tomb was actually a small room that was large enough and tall enough that the entire burial party had entered at once without stooping. It was simple inside, with a shelf of rock designed to hold the body. Once the stone was rolled into place and sealed, the airtight tomb would preserve the body for a long period of time. Such tombs were expensive, and often held several members of a family. New entrances were created over the years to add shelves for family members as needed without disturbing the original burial site.

The front stone of these tombs was often painted white—a "whited sepulcher" to which Jesus had compared the Pharisees. White on the outside, but inside full of dead men's bones. That illustration came back to Joanna as the women climbed the path past several whitewashed rocks on the way to the one that contained the body of Jesus.

The more expensive tombs were farther up the hill, and Joseph's was among the finest. The short trip took nearly an hour, as much of the walk was uphill and over rough terrain. The women talked little. Each of them walked immersed deeply in her own thoughts, yet each was also aware how good it felt to have silent company on this trip.

The closer they got to the tomb, the quicker the pace became. Each of the women was anxious that the body might have been moved or further desecrated by the Romans. They were nearly running by the time they arrived at the place where they had watched the Romans roll the stone into place on Friday.

It was the stone that first caught their eyes. Even from a distance, it was obvious that it had been moved. No guards were around. The tomb was open. By now the women were running as fast as they could, dropping strips of cloth and spilling perfume in their haste. Joanna swallowed hard. What if the Romans had stolen the body? That thought of the ultimate injustice inflicted on the One she had loved started the tears flowing again.

Suddenly, two men in clothes that gleamed like lightning appeared beside them, causing the women to fall and bow their faces to the ground in fright. None of the three dared to look up until they heard one speak in their own language, "Why do you look for the living among the dead? He is not here, He is risen! Remember how He told you, while He was still in Galilee: 'The Son of Man must be delivered into the hands of sinful men, be crucified and on the third day be raised again.'"

Joanna pressed hard against the earth still wet with the morning dew, afraid to look up into the bright light. She had heard the words before when Jesus was alive, but she never understood exactly what they meant.

Once when Jesus had said almost exactly those words, Peter had replied, "Never Lord! This shall never happen to You." Those who witnessed the exchange later told Joanna that Jesus had turned to Peter and said, "Get behind Me Satan! You are a stumbling block to Me." Few had ever seen this side of the Master, and from that time on, she had not heard anyone else question the meaning of His predictions of His death. Though no one seemed to understand it, no one had the courage to speak up after Peter's experience. It was simply another one of those unexplainable things about Jesus.

Now these two men were saying that it had occurred exactly as He said it would. The reality was beginning to sink in. He wasn't here! This wasn't a hoax. This wasn't a precautionary measure taken by the Romans. He really wasn't here! Furthermore, if He wasn't here, maybe He was alive, just as these men said.

But could it possibly be true? No prophet had ever come back from the dead. All of the great ones were dead and buried. Could it be that He was more than a prophet, Joanna wondered? Could the others have been right?

At that moment, though her eyes were squeezed tightly shut, Joanna was able to see clearly what the apostles and others would soon be allowed to see: all this had happened in order that all that was written about Him in the Law, the Prophets, and the Psalms might be fulfilled. His own words had provided the clues to what had happened, if only she had been able to understand them.

So He was the One, Joanna thought. It was the resurrection that made the difference. The prophets had possessed special powers, but none had possessed power over death. Jesus had lived a life like no one before Him, resisting the powers of sin. And now He had overcome the power of death! He was more than a prophet, He was the Son of God, and the message had been in His words all along, if only they could have understood.

Her heart leaped with joy as she scrambled to her feet in the early morning on a Judean hillside and ran after her friends. The cloth and spices and perfume were all left behind. They must tell the apostles. They wouldn't believe them at first, she thought. It would be written off as the nonsense of grieving women. But she was confident that their eyes would soon be opened too.

CHAPTER NINETEEN

READY TO DIE, SLOW TO BELIEVE

She had been through one of the most publicized trials in American history. I listened to her speak to an audience of journalists a year later about her recovery from the ordeal.

"I don't want my tombstone to read 'Rape Victim'," she said.

One apostle's name became a metaphor for skepticism because he had the bad luck to be gone when the other apostles had witnessed proof of the resurrected Jesus.

I don't know if it's on his tombstone, but he'll forever be known as "Doubting Thomas."

Earlier, he had shown his leadership and bravery by being the first to express a willingness to die for Jesus. Eventually, historians tell us, he did die for his convictions.

Yet history is not fair or kind. Thomas is not the brave leader of John 11, he's the doubter of John 20. The true Thomas, as with almost every individual, is probably somewhere in between.

He walked the roads outside Jerusalem often these days, playing the events of the last few days in his mind over and over again.

He was staying with the others whom Jesus had called to be apostles, in a modest house in Jerusalem. Occasionally he would get out from behind the locked doors to take a walk and clear his mind.

He thought about the stories about the empty tomb as he walked. Many versions of the story were circulating. Some said the Romans had moved His body to prevent someone else from stealing it. Others said some believers had taken the body to protect it. Mary and the women claimed that at the tomb they had met an angel that said He was risen.

The conflicting stories were confusing. While he wanted to believe the claims that He was alive, it was impossible to know who or what to believe.

His fellow apostles were caught up in the delusion. A few days after the crucifixion, while Thomas was on one of his walks, they claimed that He had appeared to them in the flesh. Thomas wanted to believe them in his heart, but his head wouldn't allow it.

"Unless I see the nail marks in His hands and put my finger where the nails were, and put my hand into His side, I will not believe it," he had told them. Though they had tried to convince him, they knew that they had wanted the same proof the week before. And when Jesus had offered them His hands, everyone in the room had touched them, just to make sure.

Thomas had been gone that day, alone on a walk. And he had been a loner ever since: the only one who hadn't seen Jesus.

The last time he had been with Jesus, just a few days before, He had talked like He was wanting to end His traveling and settle in one place. He spoke about a large house where they would all move, with many rooms. He said that He would go ahead of them and build it—He was, after all, a carpenter, Thomas had remembered—and that the apostles would know the way when it was completed.

Thomas had spoken up and asked, "Lord, we don't know where You are going, so how can we know the way?"

Jesus had answered him, "I am the Way and the Truth and the Life. No one comes to the Father except through Me."

Thomas hadn't asked any more questions. He still hadn't found out the way to the future house, but he had figured he would find it in time. Now, it didn't matter. The conspirators had finally won. Jesus was dead. There would be no large house with many rooms, no kingdom. Thomas had heard that some of the apostles were going back to fishing. Perhaps he would join them.

As he neared the house where they were staying, he reflected on the past three years. He had lived with Jesus and had been ready to die with Him. When Lazarus lay ill in Bethany, all the others had counseled Jesus to remain safely across the Jordan since He had nearly been stoned to death during His previous trip to Judea. Seeing that Jesus would not be persuaded to stay, Thomas had ended the debate by telling the rest, "Let us also go, that we may die with Him." They had followed his lead.

He had fully expected to die when he saw the banks of Judea come into view. But the time had not been right for the Pharisees and chief priests, and the apostles were spared. Thomas now realized that dying with Jesus then would have been easy compared to living without Him now.

He knocked on the door. It was opened just a crack, and then wide enough to let him in. He entered, turned and locked it behind him. They all felt safer that way. The religious leaders had killed Jesus and questioned Peter. Their lives could still be in danger, so they remained locked in these tight quarters. Mary and the women were bringing them food. They were all awaiting another appearance by Jesus.

Thomas wondered if their delusion of seeing Jesus wasn't a result of the claustrophobic conditions. Soon it would be time to bring up the subject of fishing with Peter and Nathanael. Perhaps James and John as well. A group this large couldn't be fed off the funds of Mary and the others for long. He was contemplating that possibility when a loud voice pierced the whispers of the room.

"Peace be with you!"

Thomas recognized the voice. It was Jesus, more radiant than in the past, standing in the middle of the room. He motioned for Thomas to come over.

Thomas pointed to his chest, gesturing as if to ask Jesus whether he was the one. But he knew he had been singled out, and he knew why. The Master was alive. And He had come to offer Thomas proof.

"Put your finger here; see My hands. Reach out your hand and put it into My side. Stop doubting and believe," He said.

Thomas was on his knees, weeping and hugging the legs of Jesus. He was ashamed and afraid to look into those eyes, but drawn to them nonetheless.

When he looked at Jesus, he saw no condemnation, only love.

"My Lord and my God!" Thomas said.

"Because you have seen Me, you have believed; blessed are those who have not seen and yet have believed," Jesus said.

The apostles came one at a time to embrace Jesus and then Thomas. They understood. Many of them had been skeptical when Mary told them of mistaking the risen Jesus for the gardener of the tombs, yet they had believed when Jesus appeared that evening and showed them His hands and His side. And now Thomas saw what they had seen a week earlier.

They would have Jesus with them for a few more days, then they would spend the rest of their lives proclaiming a resurrected Jesus to listeners who had neither seen His hands nor felt His side, but would be blessed when they believed.

And Thomas, through the risen Savior, had found the way to that large house he was seeking.

Stephen looks to heaven.

CHAPTER TWENTY

LEADING THE LAMBS HOME

My reason for writing this story, and the application of it is at the end. It is dedicated to the memory of one of my former students, Bobby James Phillips, Jr.

Speaking to this gang had always been risky. Many heretics had been beaten and jailed for what they had said to the Sanhedrin, and although he knew he was about to speak the truth, Stephen was afraid. He'd be labeled a heretic, he thought, and his fate would be the same as the other heretics.

The Sanhedrin was the highest tribunal of Judaism. Its seventy members, drawn from the priests, scribes and secular nobility of Jerusalem, were headed by the high priest. Their duty was to be the final court of appeal for all questions connected with the Mosaic law. Their decisions stood above those of the rulers of the synagogue, and served as a source of forced orthodoxy, keeping personal interpretations by priests at a minimum.

A few days before, Peter and John had spoken to the same assembly and escaped with only a night in jail after they had spoken about the resurrection of the dead. He had heard that the initial vote had been for stoning them, but that they had been spared when others in the court counseled that the movement based on the dead Teacher didn't need any more martyrs. After a harsh warning not to proclaim the risen Jesus any more, Peter and John had been released.

They had told the Sanhedrin at the time that they intended to ignore the warning, and they had. A few days later, the entire ensemble of apostles had been arrested and thrown in jail, where an angel released them during the night and ordered them to return to their preaching in the temple courts.

Frustrated by their impertinence and bewildered by their escape from prison, the Sanhedrin had decided to end this movement by putting the whole lot of them to death. Stephen remembered hearing that only the wise counsel of Gamaliel, the Sanhedrin's oldest member, had stopped the mob action. He had reminded them of other movements that had faltered on their own: Theudas, Judas the Galilean. Sooner or later, hubris got them all, and their disciples scattered.

"Leave these men alone!" he had thundered. "Let them go!" Then, lowering his voice to barely above a whisper, he added, "For if their purpose or activity is of human origin, it will fail. But if it is from God, you will not be able to stop these men; you will only find yourselves fighting against the living God."

The speech had earned the apostles a reprieve from death, but their perceived impudence also earned them a flogging before their release. They had amazed their tormentors during the beating by rejoicing in the fact that they were worthy of persecution.

In the days that followed, Gamaliel's words had nearly been prophetic as the new movement faced its first major problem. The number of followers had increased enormously; they now numbered in the thousands. In their common meals, however, the widows who were recent converts from outside the Jewish community were an ignored minority with little clout and no voice. As a result, they were being ignored in the food distribution.

To right the inequity, deacons had been established to assure that these Grecian widows were given adequate distribution of food. Stephen had been one of the seven men appointed to watch the food distribution. One of the appointees had been a Greek convert to Judaism prior to becoming a part of the Way, assuring the Grecian widows an advocate in the decision-making process. The church had avoided its first crisis.

But now Stephen faced a personal crisis. Along with his authority role as a deacon, he had been given special powers by the apostles to heal and do other miraculous signs in his ministry. His actions drew many to the Way, but eventually drew to him enemies as well. They were powerful ones, members of the Synagogue of the Freedmen, a loosely-knit synagogue of troublemakers from Cyrene, Alexandria and as far away as Cilicia and Asia. Bound together more by hate than by devotion, this group seized every opportunity to persecute those of the Way. And in their efforts they had a powerful ally, for they had the ear of the Sanhedrin.

Stephen had plenty of time to mull over the two recent brushes between the Way and the Sanhedrin in his mind as he was being led from the street where they found him performing miracles to the chamber where they would accuse him. Perhaps they would let him off with a beating as well. But what if they decided to make an example of him? Would they imprison him? Would they do even worse?

It was no surprise to Stephen that a foul mood had settled over the Sanhedrin as he was led in. They too had been thinking about the earlier confrontations with leaders of the Way. They were angered by the reports they heard. Peter and John had not been frightened by their appearance before them. In fact, they seemed all the bolder for the experience. The escape of the apostles from prison had been politically embarrassing to the Sanhedrin as well.

Furthermore, the reports of the men boasting of the beating stung the Sanhedrin members worse than any lashes on the back. These followers of Jesus must be taught somehow, and this Stephen looked to be the perfect candidate. He wasn't one of the original Twelve who had walked with the Teacher, and his death would be a clear warning to the rest without running the risk of creating a martyr.

Yes, this Stephen would do just fine.

Yet, to make this political statement to the Way, the Sanhedrin had to acquire new powers for itself. Under Roman law, the Sanhedrin did not have the right of capital punishment. They had been offered Jesus to kill, but they had declined, telling Pilate, "We have no right to execute anyone." Yet here they were, less than three full moons later, taking that power and the political risk that went with it.

To justify this dramatic precedent, the charge must be worthy of the penalty: blasphemy. "We have heard him say that this Jesus of Nazareth will destroy this place and change the customs Moses handed down to us," the accusers said. As was the custom, Stephen would be allowed to refute the charges before being sentenced, but everyone in the chamber knew what the verdict would be. The word had circulated. This one called Stephen would be killed to serve notice to the others.

But as the members of the Sanhedrin settled in for the perfunctory defense speech, many in the chamber noted that the accused man, a handsome man of about thirty years, now appeared to have the face of an angel. The description of the face of Moses as he came down the mountain from his visit with God had been a story handed down from generation to generation. At this moment, Stephen looked exactly like that description personified, a fact not lost on several in the assembly. It made them all the more ready to get rid of him. What kind of demon is this that he can take on the face of an angel?

But what they couldn't see was the transformation that took place in the mind of Stephen as his face began to glow, for Stephen was being told at that moment by God that he was not speaking for his life, he was speaking for the ages. His words on that day would not save him, but they would save others in generations to come who would listen to his simple recitation of Hebrew history in the context of God's plan.

He spoke for twenty minutes, calmly, not as one pleading for his life. Many in the Sanhedrin thought that odd; others took it as further evidence that he was a madman, making what they were about to do politically and psychologically easier for them.

It appeared that he was coming to the end of his speech. They could get on to what they had to do. Yet he had not yet incriminated himself. If there was to be a killing, there had to be blasphemy. He had traced the history of the Israelite nation through the building of the temple, and now he stood there telling them that God didn't want to dwell in that house or any other made by man.

There it was! Blasphemy worthy of death! For if God didn't live in the temple, He didn't live at all. Enough of this, he's ours now! We don't have to listen to any more.

But Stephen continued. He accused them, the most holy elect of Judaism, of killing both the prophets and the Righteous One about whom the prophets had prophesied. The room became a sea of clicking noises as the assembled men began to gnash their teeth at him. This sign of Jewish disfavor was accomplished by opening and closing the jaws quickly, making the teeth click. It was an unpleasant sound to the ears and a symbol of displeasure. The clicks turned to shouts as Stephen began to tell the Sanhedrin his valedictory vision of Jesus standing at the right hand of God.

But Stephen didn't hear their vocal displeasure. By now his ears were tuned only to the eternal voices, the ones calling him home.

Stephen was dragged out of town and stoned to death on that day. But Stephen was a spectator of his death, not a suffering participant. The recorded account of his death speaks only of his praying, not of his suffering. Heaven had already opened to him while he was still in the chamber of the Sanhedrin, and when he fell asleep a few minutes later, he did so without feeling a stone.

Yesterday, I attended the funeral of one of my favorite former students and his younger brother. Their deaths were senseless and brutal murders that brought their community to a virtual standstill days before Christmas. The funeral was a testament to their lives. The overflow crowd filled the building and its lobby, and scores more stood in the cold December air on the church lawn just to be near the memorial service.

One of the ministers read the story above to the crowd and said, "I don't think God lets His lambs suffer. When the blows began, God took Bobby away, just like He took Stephen away."

I remember thinking precisely the same thing when I was eight years old and heard that my uncle, a minister, had died a few hours after a car wreck. He probably watched those last attempts to revive him from the opening of heaven, I thought.

In the years since, I haven't worked out all of the theology on that belief, but I do know two things. First, we are already eternal beings, we just haven't "metamorphosed" yet. Second, we are headed to a place where there is no more pain or tears. And if God wants to blur the lines of eternity to ease the pain of a few lambs like Stephen, Bobby and my uncle, that's fine with me.